The Way to God

(AND HOW TO FIND IT)

ANEKO
PRESS

We love hearing from our readers. Please contact us at www.anekopress.com/questions-comments with any questions, comments, or suggestions.

Printed in Hong Kong
Aneko Press
www.anekopress.com
Aneko Press, Life Sentence Publishing, and our logos are trademarks of
Life Sentence Publishing, Inc.
203 E. Birch Street
P.O. Box 652
Abbotsford, WI 54405

RELIGION / Christian Ministry / Evangelism
Paperback ISBN: 978-1-62245-454-9
eBook ISBN: 978-1-62245-455-6

10 9 8 7 6 5 4

Available where books are sold

Contents

To the Reader

I have attempted to point the way to God in this small volume. I have included a large part of several sermons, which I preached in different cities in Great Britain and my own country – the United States. God graciously blessed these sermons, when I preached them from the pulpit, and I pray that He will add His blessing on them now in their printed form along with some additional material.

I call attention first to the love of God, the source of all gifts of grace. Then, I try to present truths to meet the specific needs of different groups of people, answering how a person can be right with God and hoping to lead souls to Him who is *the way, the truth, and the life* (John 14:6).

The last chapter is specially addressed to backsliders – a class of people who are far too numerous among us.

With earnest prayer and hope that by the blessing of God on these pages, the reader may be strengthened, established, and settled in the faith of Christ,

I am yours in His service,

Dwight Moody

Chapter 1

Love That Passes
All Knowledge

To know the love of Christ which surpasses knowledge. (Ephesians 3:19)

I f I could only make people understand the real meaning of the words of the apostle John – *God is love* – I would take that single text and go up and down the world proclaiming this glorious truth. If you can convince someone that you love him, you have won his heart. If we can convince people to believe that God loves them, we would find them crowding into the kingdom of heaven. The trouble is that people think God hates them, and so they are constantly running from Him.

We built a church in Chicago some years ago and were very anxious to teach the people the love of God. We thought that if we could not preach it into their hearts, we would try to emphasize it other ways; so we put these words right over the pulpit: *God is love*. A man going along the streets one night glanced through the door and saw the text. He was a poor prodigal who had wandered away from God. As he walked by, he thought to himself, *God is love! No! He does not love me, for I am a poor miserable sinner.* He tried to get the text out of his mind, but it seemed to stand out right before him in letters of fire. He went on a little farther, then turned around, came back, and went into the meeting.

He did not hear the sermon, but the words of that short text had been deeply lodged in his heart, and that was enough. It is of little account what men say, if only the Word of God gets an entrance into the sinner's heart. That man stayed after the first meeting was over, and I found him there weeping like a child. I unfolded the Scriptures and told him how God had loved him all the time, even though he had wandered so far away, and that God waited to receive him and forgive him. The light of the gospel broke into his mind, and he went away a new man, rejoicing in the love of Christ Jesus.

There is nothing in this world that we prize as much as love. Show me a person who has no one to care for him or love him, and I will show you one of the most wretched beings on the face of the earth. Why do people commit suicide? Very often it is because this thought steals in upon them – that no one loves them, and they would rather die than live.

I know of no truth in the whole Bible that ought to come home to us with such power and tenderness as that of the love of God, and there is no truth in the Bible that Satan would so much like to blot out. For more than six thousand years, he has been trying to persuade people that God does not love them. He succeeded in making our first parents believe this lie, and he too often succeeds with their children.

The idea that God does not love us often comes from false teaching. Parents make a mistake in teaching children that God only loves them when they do right but does not love them when they do wrong. You do not teach your children that you hate them when they do wrong. Their wrongdoing does not change your love into hate; if it did, you would change your love a great many times. Because your child is grouchy or has committed some act of disobedience, you do not cast him out as though he did not belong to you! No! He is still your child and you love him. If some people have gone astray from God, it does not mean that He hates them. It is the sin, the unrepentance, the wicked heart that He hates. *But God demonstrates His own love toward us, in that while we were yet sinners, Christ died for us* (Romans 5:8). *We love, because He first loved us* (1 John 4:19).

> There is a vast difference between human love and divine love.

I believe the reason many people think God does not love them is that they are measuring God by their own small rule, from their own standpoint. We love others as long as we consider them worthy of our love; when they are not, we cast them off. It is not so with God. There is a vast difference between human love and divine love.

Ephesians 3:18 tells us about the breadth and length and depth and height of God's love. Many of us think we know something of God's love, but centuries from now we will admit we only knew a small part of it. Columbus discovered America, but what did he know about its great lakes, rivers, forests, and the Mississippi Valley? He died without knowing much about what he had discovered. In the same way, many of us have discovered something of the love of God, but there are heights, depths, and lengths of it we do not know. That love is a great ocean, and we must plunge into it before we really know anything of it.

A Roman Catholic archbishop of Paris was thrown into prison and condemned to be shot. A little while before he was led out to die, he saw a window in his cell in the shape of a cross. On the top of the cross he wrote *height*, at the bottom *depth*, and at the end of each arm *length*. He had experienced the truth conveyed in the Isaac Watts' hymn:

> When I survey the wondrous cross
> > On which the Prince of glory died,
> My richest gain I count but loss,
> > And pour contempt on all my pride.
>
> Forbid it, Lord, that I should boast,
> > Save in the death of Christ my God!
> All the vain things that charm me most,
> > I sacrifice them to His blood.
>
> See from His head, His hands, His feet,
> > Sorrow and love flow mingled down!
> Did e'er such love and sorrow meet,
> > Or thorns compose so rich a crown?

Were the whole realm of nature mine,
    That were a present far too small;
Love so amazing, so divine,
    Demands my soul, my life, my all.

When we wish to know the love of God, we should go to Calvary. Can we look upon that scene and say God did not love us? That cross speaks of the love of God. Greater love has never been taught than that which the cross teaches. What prompted God to give up Christ and what prompted Christ to die, if it were not love? *Greater love has no one than this, that one lay down his life for his friends* (John 15:13). Christ laid down His life for His enemies. Christ laid down His life for His murderers. Christ laid down His life for those who hated Him. The spirit of the cross, the spirit of Calvary, is love. When they were mocking Him and deriding Him, what did He say? *Father, forgive them; for they do not know what they are doing* (Luke 23:34). That is love. He did not call down fire from heaven to consume them; there was nothing but love in His heart.

God's Love Is Unchangeable

If you study the Bible, you will find that the love of God is unchangeable. Many who loved you at one time have perhaps grown cold in their affection and turned away from you: it may be that their love is changed to hatred. It is not so with God. It is recorded of Jesus Christ, just when He was about to be parted from His disciples and led away to Calvary, that *having loved His own who were in the world, He loved them to the end* (John 13:1). He knew that one of His disciples would betray Him, yet He loved Judas. He knew that another disciple would deny Him and swear that he never knew Him, and yet He loved Peter. Christ had the love for Peter that broke Peter's heart and brought him back in repentance to the feet of his Lord. For three years, Jesus had been with the disciples, teaching them His love, not only by His life and words but also by His works. On the night of His betrayal, He took a basin of water, wrapped Himself with a towel, took the place of a servant, and washed their feet. He wanted to convince them of His unchanging love.

There is no portion of Scripture I read as often as John 14, and there is none that I love more. I never tire of reading it. Hear what our Lord says, as He pours out His heart to His disciples: *In that day you will know that I am in My Father, and you in Me, and I in you. He who has My commandments and keeps them is the one who loves Me; and he who loves Me will be loved by My Father* (John 14:20-21). Think of the great God who created heaven and earth loving you and me! *If anyone loves Me, he will keep My word; and My Father will love him, and We will come to him and make Our abode with him* (John 14:23).

Would to God that our puny minds could grasp this great truth – the Father and the Son so love us that they desire to come and abide with us! Not to stay for a night, but to come and abide in our hearts.

We have another wonderful passage in John 17:23: *I in them and You in Me, that they may be perfected in unity, so that the world may know that You sent Me, and loved them, even as You have loved Me.* I think that is one of the most remarkable sayings that ever fell from the lips of Jesus Christ. There is no reason the Father should not love Him. He was obedient unto death. He never transgressed the Father's law or turned aside from the path of perfect obedience by one hair's breadth. It is very different with us, and yet notwithstanding all our rebellion and foolishness, He says that if we are trusting in Christ, the Father loves us as He loves the Son. Marvelous love! Wonderful love! That God can possibly love us as He loves His own Son seems too good to be true, yet that is what Jesus Christ teaches.

> God's love is not only unchangeable, but it is unfailing.

It is hard to make a sinner believe in this unchangeable love of God. When someone has wandered away from God, he thinks that God hates him. We must make a distinction between sin and the sinner. God loves the sinner, but He hates the sin.[1] He hates sin because it mars human life. It is because God loves the sinner that He hates sin.

God's Love Is Unfailing

God's love is not only unchangeable, but it is unfailing.

---

1   As much as this is scriptural, there is also scripture that indicates God's hatred of sinners, such as Psalm 5:5: *The boastful shall not stand in Your sight; You hate all workers of iniquity,* and Psalm 7:11: *The foolish (those who are governed by carnal thoughts or desires) shall not stand in thy sight; thou dost hate all workers of iniquity.*

In Isaiah 49:15-16 we read: *Can a woman forget her nursing child and have no compassion on the son of her womb? Even these may forget, but I will not forget you. Behold, I have inscribed you on the palms of My hands; Your walls are continually before Me.*

The strongest human love that we know of is a mother's love. Many things will separate a man from his wife. A father may turn his back on his child. Brothers and sisters may become bitter enemies. Husbands may desert their wives and wives may desert their husbands, but a mother's love endures through all. In good repute, in bad repute, in the face of the world's condemnation, a mother loves on and hopes that her child may turn from his evil ways and repent. She remembers the infant smiles, the merry laugh of childhood, the promise of youth; she can never be brought to think him unworthy. Death cannot quench a mother's love; it is stronger than death.

You have seen a mother watching over her sick child. How willingly she would take the disease into her own body if her child could be made well! Week after week she will keep watch; she will let no one else take care of that sick child.

A friend of mine, some time ago, was visiting in a beautiful home where he met a number of friends. After they had all gone away, having left something behind, he went back to get it. There he found the lady of the house, a wealthy lady, sitting behind a poor fellow who looked like a tramp. He was her own son. Like the prodigal, he had wandered far away, yet the mother said, "This is my boy; I love him still." Take a mother with nine or ten children, and if one goes astray, she seems to love that one more than any of the rest.

A leading minister in the state of New York once told me of a father who was a very bad person. The mother did all she could to prevent her son from following in the sinful ways of his father, but the influence of the father was stronger. He led his son into all kinds of sin until the lad became one of the worst of criminals. He committed murder and was put on trial. All through the trial, the widowed mother (for the father had died) sat in the court. When the witnesses testified against the boy, it seemed to hurt the mother much more than the son. When he was found guilty and sentenced to die, everyone else felt the justice of the verdict and seemed satisfied at the result. But the mother's love never faltered. She begged for a reprieve, but that was denied. After the execution, she asked for her son's body so she could bury him, and this also was refused. According to custom, he was buried in the prison yard. A little while afterwards, the mother herself died, but before she died, she expressed a desire to be buried by the side of her boy. She was not ashamed of being known as the mother of a murderer.

Another story is told of a young woman in Scotland who left her home and became an outcast in Glasgow. Her mother sought her far and wide but in vain. At last, she caused her own picture to be hung upon the walls of the Midnight Mission rooms, where abandoned women sometimes stayed. Many women gave the picture a passing glance, but one young woman lingered by the picture. The young woman recognized the same dear face that looked down upon her in her childhood. She had not forgotten nor cast off her sinning child, or her picture would never have been hung upon those walls. The lips seemed to open and whisper, "Come home; I forgive you and love you still." The poor girl sank down, overwhelmed with her feelings. She was the prodigal daughter. The sight of her mother's face had broken her heart. She became truly penitent for her sins, and with a heart full of sorrow and shame, she returned to her forsaken home, and mother and daughter were once more united.

But let me tell you that no mother's love is to be compared with the love of God; it does not measure up to the height or the depth of God's love. No mother in this world ever loved her child as God loves you and me. Think of the love that God must have had when He gave His Son to die for the world. I used to think a good deal more of Christ than I did of the Father. Somehow or other I had the idea that God was a stern judge and that Christ came between me and God and appeased the anger of God. But after I became a father and for years had an only son, as I looked at my boy, I thought of the Father giving His Son to die, and it seemed as if it required more love for the Father to give His Son than for the Son to die.

Oh, the love that God must have had for the world when He gave His Son to die for it! *God so loved the world, that He gave His only begotten Son, that whoever believes in Him shall not perish, but have eternal life* (John 3:16). I have never been able to preach from that text. I have often thought I would, but it is so high that I can never climb to its height. I have just quoted it and moved on. Who can fathom the depth of those words: *God so loved the world*? We can never scale the heights of His love or fathom its depths. Paul prayed that he might know the height, the depth, the length, and the breadth of the love of God, but it was past his finding out. It *surpasses knowledge* (Ephesians 3:19).

Nothing speaks to us of the love of God like the cross of Christ. Come with me to Calvary and look upon the Son of God as He hangs there. Can you hear that piercing cry from His dying lips, *Father, forgive them; for they do not know what they are doing*, and say that He does not love you? *Greater love has no one than this, that one lay down his life for his friends* (John 15:13). But Jesus Christ laid down His life for His enemies.

> Nothing speaks to us of the love of God like the cross of Christ.

Another thought is this: He loved us long before we ever thought of Him. The idea that He does not love us until we first love Him is not to be found in Scripture. In 1 John 4:10, it is written: *In this is love, not that we loved God, but that He loved us and sent His Son to be the propitiation for our sins.* He loved us before we ever thought of loving Him. You loved your children before they knew anything about your love. And so, long before we ever thought of God, we were in His thoughts.

What brought the prodigal home? It was the thought that his father loved him. Suppose the news had reached him that he was cast off and that his father did not care for him anymore; would he have gone back? Never! But the thought dawned upon him that his father loved him still; so he rose up and went back to his home.

Dear reader, the love of the Father ought to bring us back to Him. It was Adam's calamity and sin that revealed God's love. When Adam fell, God came down and dealt in mercy with him. If anyone is lost, it will not be because God does not love him; it will be because he has resisted the love of God.

What will make heaven attractive? Is it the pearly gates or the golden street? No. Heaven will be attractive because there we will behold Him who loved us so much as to give His only begotten Son to die for us. What makes home attractive? Is it the beautiful furniture and stately rooms? No. Some homes with all these are like whited sepulchres. In Brooklyn a mother was dying, and it was necessary to take her child from her because the little child could not understand the nature of the sickness, and she did not ever want to leave her mother alone. Every night, the child sobbed herself to sleep in a neighbor's house, because she wanted to go back to her mother's house; but the mother grew worse, and they could not take the child home. At last the mother died. After her death they thought it best not to let the child see her dead mother in her coffin. After the burial, the child ran into one room crying, "Mama! Mama!" and then into another crying, "Mama! Mama!" and so she went over the whole house; when the little child failed to find that loved one at home, she cried to be taken back to the neighbors. So what makes heaven attractive is the thought that we will see Christ Jesus, who has loved us and given Himself for us.

If you ask me why God loves us, I cannot tell. I suppose it is because He is a true Father. It is His nature to love, just as it is the nature of the sun to shine. He wants you to share in that love. Do not let unbelief keep you away from Him. Do not think that because you are a sinner, God does not love you or care for you. He does! He wants to save you and bless you.

For while we were still helpless, at the right time Christ died for the ungodly (Romans 5:6). Is that not enough to convince you that He loves you? He would not have died for you if He had not loved you. Is your heart so hard that you can brace yourself up against His love and spurn and despise it? You *can* do it, but it will be at your peril.

I can imagine some saying to themselves, "Yes, we believe that God loves us, if we love Him; we believe that God loves the pure and the holy." Let me say, my friend, not only does God love the pure and the holy, but He also loves us when we are still ungodly. *But God demonstrates His own love toward us, in that while we were yet sinners, Christ died for us* (Romans 5:8). God sent Him to die for the sins of the world. If you belong to the world, then you may have part and lot in this love that has been exhibited in the cross of Christ.

Revelation 1:5 means a great deal to me: *To Him who loves us and released us from our sins by His blood.* It might be thought that God would first wash us and then love us. But no, He first loved us. About eight years ago, the whole country was intensely excited about Charlie

Ross, a four-year-old child, who was kidnapped. Two men in a one-horse carriage asked him and an older brother if they wanted some candy. They then drove away with the younger boy, leaving the older one. For many years a search has been made in every state and territory. Men have been over to Great Britain, France, and Germany and have hunted in vain for the child. The mother still lives in the hope that she will see her long lost Charlie. I do not remember the whole country to have been so disturbed about any event, unless it was the assassination of President Garfield.

Well, suppose the mother of Charlie Ross was sitting on the platform at a meeting, and while the preacher was speaking, she happened to look in the audience and see her long lost son. Suppose he was poor, dirty and ragged, shoeless and coatless; what would she do? Would she wait till he was washed and decently clothed before she would acknowledge him? No, she would get off the platform at once, rush towards him, and take him in her arms. After that, she would wash and clothe him. So it is with God. He loved us and washed us. I can imagine someone asking, "If God loves me, why does He not make me good?" God wants sons and daughters in heaven; He does not want machines or slaves. He could break our stubborn hearts, but He wants to draw us towards Himself by the cords of love.

He wants you to sit down with Him at the marriage supper of the Lamb. He wants to wash you and make you whiter than snow. He wants you to walk with Him on the crystal pavement of heaven – that distant blissful world. He wants to adopt you into His family and make you a son or a daughter of heaven. Will you trample His love under your feet, or will you give yourself to Him once and for all?

When the terrible Civil War was going on, a mother received the news that her boy had been wounded in the Battle of the Wilderness. She took the first train and headed out to see her boy, although the order had gone forth from the War Department that no more women should be admitted within the lines. But a mother's love knows nothing about orders, so she managed by tears and entreaties to get through the lines. At last she found the hospital where her boy was. Then she went to the doctor and she said, "Will you let me go to the ward and take care of my boy?"

> Will you trample His love under your feet?

The doctor said, "I just got your boy to sleep; he is in a very critical state, and I am afraid if you wake him up, the excitement will be so great that it will kill him. You had better wait a while and remain outside until I tell him that you have come; let me break the news to him gradually."

The mother looked into the doctor's face and said, "Doctor, suppose my boy does not wake up, and I should never again see him alive! Let me go and sit down by his side; I won't speak to him."

"If you will not speak to him, you may do so," said the doctor.

She crept to the cot and looked into the face of her boy. How she had longed to look at him! How her eyes

seemed to be feasting as she gazed upon his counte-
nance! When she got near enough, she could not keep
her hands off; she laid that tender, loving hand upon
his brow. The moment the hand touched the forehead
of her boy, without opening his eyes, he cried out,
"Mother, you have come!" He knew the touch of that
loving hand. There was love and sympathy in it.

Ah, sinner, if you feel the loving touch of Jesus, you
will recognize it; it is full of tenderness. The world may
treat you unkindly, but Christ never will. You will never
have a better friend in this world. What you need is to
come to Him today. Let His loving arm be under you;
let His loving hand be about you. He will hold you with
mighty power. He will keep you and fill your heart with
His tenderness and love.

I can imagine some of you asking, "How should I
go to Him?" Why, just as you would go to your mother.
Have you done your mother a great injury and a great
wrong? If so, go to her and say, "Mother, I want you to
forgive me." Treat Christ in the same way. Go to Him
today and tell Him that you have not loved Him, that
you have not treated Him right; confess your sins and
see how quickly He will bless you.

I am reminded of another incident – that of a boy
who had been tried by court-martial and ordered to be
shot. The hearts of the father and mother were broken
when they heard the news. In that home was a little girl.
She had read the life of Abraham Lincoln, and she said,
"If Abraham Lincoln knew how much my father and
mother loved their boy, he would not let my brother
be shot." She wanted her father to go to Washington to

plead for his boy. But the father said, "No; there is no use; the law must take its course. They have refused to pardon one or two who have been sentenced by that court-martial, and an order has gone forth that the president is not going to interfere again; if a man has been sentenced by court-martial, he must suffer the consequences." That father and mother did not have faith to believe that their boy might be pardoned.

But the little girl was strong in hope; she got on the train way up in Vermont and started toward Washington. When she reached the White House, the soldiers refused to let her in, but she told her pitiful story, and they allowed her to pass. When she got to the secretary's room where the president's private secretary was, he refused to allow her to enter the private office of the president. But the little girl told her story, and it touched the heart of the private secretary, so he allowed her in. As she went into Abraham Lincoln's room, United States senators, generals, governors, and leading politicians were there to discuss important business concerning the war, but President Lincoln happened to see that child standing at his door. He wanted to know what she wanted, and she went right to him and told her story in her own language. He was a father, and the great tears trickled down Abraham Lincoln's cheeks. He wrote a dispatch and sent it to the army to have that boy sent to Washington at once. When he arrived, the president pardoned him, gave him thirty days furlough, and sent him home with the little girl to cheer the hearts of the father and mother.

Do you want to know how to go to Christ? Go just

as that little girl went to Abraham Lincoln. It may be possible that you have a dark story to tell. Let it all out; keep nothing back. If Abraham Lincoln had compassion on that little girl and heard her petition and answered it, do you think the Lord Jesus will not hear your prayer? Do you think that Abraham Lincoln, or any man who ever lived on earth, had as much compassion as Christ? No! He will be moved with compassion when no one else will. He will have mercy when no one else will. He will have pity when no one else will. If you will go right to Him, confessing your sin and your need, He will save you.

A few years ago, a man left England and went to America. He was an Englishman, but he was naturalized to become an American citizen. After a few years, he felt restless and dissatisfied, so he went to Cuba. After he had been in Cuba a while, civil war broke out there. This was in 1867, and the man was arrested by the Spanish government as a spy. He was tried by court-martial, found guilty, and ordered to be shot. The whole trial was conducted in the Spanish language, and the poor man did not know what was going on.

When they told him the verdict, that he was found guilty and had been condemned to be shot, he sent to the American and English embassies and laid the whole case before them, proving his innocence and claiming protection. They examined the case and found that this man, whom the Spanish officers had condemned to be shot, was perfectly innocent. They went to the Spanish general and said, "Look here, this man whom you have condemned to death is an innocent man; he is not guilty."

But the Spanish general said, "He has been tried by our law. He has been found guilty, and he must die." There was no electric cable to send a telegraph, and so these men could not consult with their governments.

The morning came on which the man was to be executed. He was brought out in a cart, sitting on his coffin, and he was taken to the place where he was to be executed. A grave was dug. They took the coffin out of the cart, placed the young man upon it, and pulled a black hood down over his face. The Spanish soldiers awaited the order to fire, but just then the American and English consuls rode up. The English consul sprang out of the carriage and took the Union Jack, the British flag, and

Believe it today; receive it into your heart and enter into a new life.

wrapped it around the man, and the American consul wrapped the Star-Spangled Banner around him; then turning to the Spanish officers, they said, "Fire upon those flags if you dare." They did not dare to fire upon the flags. There were two great governments behind those flags. That was the secret of it.

He has brought me to his banquet hall, and his banner over me is love. . . . His left hand be under my head and his right hand embrace me (Song of Solomon 2:4, 6). Thank God we can come under the banner today if we will. Any poor sinner can come under that banner today. His banner of love is over us. Blessed gospel; blessed, precious news. Believe it today; receive it into your heart and enter into a new life. Let the love of God be shed abroad in your heart by the Holy Spirit today (Romans 5:5). It will drive away darkness. It will drive away gloom. It will drive away sin, and peace and joy will be yours.

Chapter 2

The Gateway into the Kingdom

Unless one is born again he cannot see the kingdom of God. (John 3:3)

This passage may be the most familiar portion of the Word of God that we know. I suppose if I asked those in any audience if they believed that Jesus Christ taught the doctrine of the new birth, nine-tenths of them would say, "Yes, I believe He did."

The words of this text embody one of the most solemn questions that can come before us. We can afford to be deceived about many things, but not about this. Christ makes it very plain. He says, *Unless one is born again he cannot see the kingdom of God.* This doctrine of the new birth is therefore the foundation of all our hopes for the world to come. It is really the ABCs of the Christian religion. My experience has been that if someone is unsound on this doctrine, he will be unsound on almost every other fundamental doctrine in the Bible. A true understanding of this subject will help a person solve a thousand difficulties that he may meet with in the Word of God. Things that seemed very dark and mysterious before will become very plain.

The doctrine of the new birth upsets all false religion – all false views about the Bible and about God. A friend of mine once told me that in one of his meetings after the service, a man came to him with a long list of questions written out for him to answer. He said, "If you can answer these questions satisfactorily, I have made up my mind to become a Christian."

"Do you not think," said my friend, "that you had better come to Christ first? Then you can look into these questions." The man thought that perhaps he had better do so. After he had received Christ, he looked again at his list of questions, but then it seemed to him as if they had all been answered.

Nicodemus came with his troubled mind, and Christ said to him, *You must be born again.* He was treated altogether differently from what he had expected, but I think that was the most blessed night in all his life. To be born again is the greatest blessing that will ever come to us in this world.

Notice how Scripture puts it. *Unless one is born again*, or born of the Spirit. From among a number of other passages where we find this word *unless*, I would just name three. *Unless you repent, you will all likewise perish* (Luke 13:3, 5). *Unless you are converted and become like children, you will not enter the kingdom of heaven* (Matthew 18:3). *Unless your righteousness*

*surpasses that of the scribes and Pharisees, you will not
enter the kingdom of heaven* (Matthew 5:20). They all
really mean the same thing.

I am so thankful that our Lord spoke of the new
birth to this ruler of the Jews, this doctor of the law,
rather than to the woman at the well of Samaria, or
to Matthew the publican, or to
Zacchaeus. If He had reserved
His teaching on this great matter for these three, or such as
these, people would have said,
"Oh yes, these publicans and
harlots need to be converted,
but I am an upright man. I do
not need to be converted." I suppose Nicodemus was
one of the best specimens of the people of Jerusalem;
there was nothing on record against him.

> I think it is hardly
> necessary for me to
> prove that we need to
> be born again before
> we are fit for heaven.

I think it is hardly necessary for me to prove that
we need to be born again before we are fit for heaven. I
dare say that there is no honest man who would say he
is ready for the kingdom of God until he is born of the
Holy Spirit. The Bible teaches us that man by nature is
lost and guilty, and our experience confirms this. We
know also that the best and holiest man will very soon
fall into sin if he turns away from God.

Now, let me say what regeneration is not. It is not
going to church. Very often when I see people, I ask
them if they are Christians. "Yes, of course I am; I go to
church every Sunday." Ah, but this is not regeneration.

Others say, "I am trying to do what is right – am I
not a Christian? Isn't that a new birth?" No. What has

that to do with being born again? There is yet another class – those who have "turned over a new leaf" and think they are regenerated. No, forming a new resolution is not being born again.

Nor will being baptized do you any good. Yet you hear people say, "Why, I have been baptized, and I was born again when I was baptized." They believe that because they were baptized into the church, they were baptized into the kingdom of God. I tell you that it is utterly impossible. You may be baptized into the church and yet not be baptized into the Son of God. Baptism is all right in its place. God forbid that I should say anything against it. But if you put that in the place of regeneration – in the place of the new birth – it is a terrible mistake. You cannot be baptized into the kingdom of God. *Unless one is born again he cannot see the kingdom of God.* If anyone reading this rests his hopes on anything else – on any other foundation – I pray that God may sweep it away.

Another class says, "I go to the Lord's Supper; I regularly partake of the sacrament." Blessed ordinance! Jesus has said that as often as you do it, you remember His death. Yet that is not being born again; that is not passing from death unto life. Jesus says plainly, and so plainly that there shouldn't be any mistake about it, *Unless one is born again he cannot see the kingdom of God.* What has a sacrament to do with that? What has going to church to do with being born again?

Another person comes up and says, "I say my prayers regularly." Still, I say that is not being born of the Spirit. It is a very solemn question then, that comes up before us, and every reader should ask himself earnestly and faithfully, "Have I been born again? Have I been born of the Spirit? Have I passed from death unto life?"

One group of people says that special religious meetings are very good for some people. They would be very good if you could get the drunkard there, or get the gambler there, or get other vicious people there – that would do a great deal of good. But, "We don't need to be converted," they say. To whom did Christ utter these words of wisdom? To Nicodemus. Who was Nicodemus? Was he a drunkard, a gambler, or a thief? No! No doubt he was one of the very best men in Jerusalem. He was an honorable leader. He belonged to the Sanhedrin. He held a very high position. He was a devout man. He was one of the very wisest men. And yet what did Christ say to him? *Unless one is born again he cannot see the kingdom of God.*

But I can imagine someone saying, "What am I to do? I cannot create life. I certainly cannot save myself." You certainly cannot, and we do not claim that you can. We tell you it is utterly impossible to make anyone better without Christ, but that is what people are trying to do. They are trying to patch up this "old Adam" nature. However, there must be a new creation. Regeneration is a new creation, and if it is a new creation, it must be the work of God. In the first chapter of Genesis, humans do not appear. There is no one there but God. Man is not there to take part. When God created the earth, He was alone. When Christ redeemed the world, He was alone.

That which is born of the flesh is flesh, and that which

is born of the Spirit is spirit (John 3:6). The Ethiopian cannot change his skin, and the leopard cannot change his spots (Jeremiah 13:23). You might as well try to make yourselves pure and holy without the help of God. It would be just as easy for you to do that as for a person to change the color of his skin. A man might just as well try to leap over the moon as to serve God in the flesh. Therefore, *That which is born of the flesh is flesh, and that which is born of the Spirit is spirit* (John 3:6).

God tells us in this chapter how we are to get into His kingdom. We are not to work our way in, although salvation would be worth working for, if it were possible. We all admit that. If there were rivers and mountains in the way, it would be worthwhile to swim those rivers and climb those mountains. There is no doubt that salvation would be worth all that effort, but we do not obtain it by our works. It is *to the one who does not work, but believes* (Romans 4:5). We work because we are saved; we do not work to be saved. We work from the cross but not towards it. It is written to work out your own salvation *with fear and trembling* (Philippians 2:12). You must have your salvation before you can work it out.

> We work because we are saved; we do not work to be saved.

Suppose I say to my little boy, "I want you to spend that hundred dollars carefully."

"Well," he says, "let me have the hundred dollars, and I will be careful how I spend it."

I remember when I first left home and went to Boston. I had spent all my money, and I went to the post office three times a day. I knew that the mail from home only arrived once a day, but I thought by some possibility there might be a letter for me. At last I received a letter from my little sister, and oh, how glad I was to get it. She had heard that there were a great many pickpockets in Boston, and a large part of that letter was to urge me to be very careful not to let anybody pick my pocket. However, I needed to have something in my pocket before I could have it picked. So you must have salvation before you can work it out.

When Christ cried out on Calvary, "It is finished!" He meant what He said. All that people have to do now is just to accept the work of Jesus Christ. There is no hope for man or woman as long as they are trying to work out salvation for themselves. I can imagine there are some people who will say, as Nicodemus possibly did, "This is a very mysterious thing." I see the scowl on that Pharisee's brow as he says, "How can these things be?" It sounds very strange to his ear. "Born again; born of the Spirit! How can these things be?"

A great many people say, "You must reason it out; if you don't reason it out, don't ask us to believe it." I can imagine many people saying that. When you ask me to reason it out, I tell you sincerely I cannot do it. *The wind blows where it wishes and you hear the sound of it, but do not know where it comes from and where it is going; so is everyone who is born of the Spirit* (John 3:8). I don't understand everything about the wind. You ask me to reason it out. I cannot. It may blow due north here, and a hundred miles away due south. I may go up a few hundred feet and find it blowing in an entirely opposite direction from what it is down here. You ask me to explain these currents of wind, but what if I cannot explain them and do not understand them, but I take my stand and declare, "There is no such thing as wind."

I can imagine some little girl saying, "I know more about it than that man does; I have often heard the wind and felt it blowing against my face." She might ask, "Didn't the wind blow my umbrella out of my hands the other day? Didn't I see it blow a man's hat off in the street? Haven't I seen it blow the trees in the forest and the growing corn in the country?"

You might just as well tell me that there is no such thing as wind as tell me there is no such thing as a person being born of the Spirit. I have felt the Spirit of God working in my heart, just as really and as truly as I have felt the wind blowing in my face. I cannot reason it out. There are a great many things I cannot reason out, but which I believe. I never could reason out the creation. I can see the world, but I cannot tell how God made it out of nothing. But almost everyone will admit there is a creative power.

There are a great many things that I cannot explain and cannot reason out, and yet I believe. I heard a commercial traveler say that he had heard that the ministry and religion of Jesus Christ were matters of revelation and not of investigation. *But when God . . . was pleased to reveal his Son in me*, says Paul (Galatians 1:15-16). There was a party of young men, going to the country together; on their journey they made up their minds not to believe anything they could not reason out. An old man heard them, and he said to them, "I heard you say you would not believe anything you could not reason out."

"Yes," they said, "that is so."

"Well," he said, "coming down on the train today, I noticed some geese, some sheep, some swine, and some cattle all eating grass. Can you tell me by what process that same grass was turned into hair, feathers, bristles, and wool? Do you believe it is a fact?"

"Oh yes," they said. "We cannot help believing that, though we fail to understand it."

"Well," said the old man, "I cannot help believing in Jesus Christ."

And I cannot help believing in the regeneration of man, when I see people who have been reclaimed, when I see people who have been reformed, changed by God and given new hearts by God's Holy Spirit. Haven't some of the very worst people been regenerated – picked up out of the pit with their feet set upon the Rock and a new song put in their mouths? Their tongues used to curse and blaspheme, but now they praise God. *Old things passed away; behold, new things have come* (2 Corinthians 5:17). They are not only reformed, but they are regenerated. They are new creations in Christ Jesus.

> I think if you want to get near hell, you should go to a poor drunkard's home.

Down there in the dark alleys of one of our great cities is a poor drunkard. I think if you want to get near hell, you should go to a poor drunkard's home.

Go to the house of that poor miserable drunkard. Is there anything more like hell on earth? See the want and distress that reign there. But listen! A footstep is heard at the door, and the children run and hide. The patient wife waits to meet the man. He has been her torment. Many times she has been the recipient of his anger. Many times that strong right hand has been brought down on her defenseless head. And now she waits, expecting to hear his oaths and suffer his brutal treatment. He comes in and says to her, "I have been to the meeting, and I heard there that if I turn to God, I can be converted. I believe that God is able to save me."

Go down to that house again in a few weeks. What a change! As you approach, you hear someone singing. It is not the song of a partygoer but the sound of that good old hymn, "Rock of Ages." The children are no longer afraid of the man but gather around his knee. His wife is near him, her face lit up with a happy glow. Isn't that a picture of regeneration? I can take you to many such homes, made happy by the regenerating power of the gospel of Christ. What people need is the power to overcome temptation, the power to lead a right life – and that power is found in God's Holy Spirit.

The only way to get into the kingdom of God is to be *born* into it. The law of this country requires that the president should be born in the country. When foreigners come to our shores, they have no right to complain against such a law that forbids them from ever becoming the president. Now, hasn't God a right to make a law that all those who become heirs of eternal life must be *born* into His kingdom?

Someone who has not been born again would rather be in hell than in heaven. Take a man whose heart is full of corruption and wickedness and place him in heaven among the pure, the holy, and the redeemed; he would not want to stay there. Certainly, if we are to be happy in heaven, we must begin to make a heaven here on earth. Heaven is a prepared place for a prepared people. If a gambler or a blasphemer were taken out of the streets of New York and placed on the crystal pavement of heaven and under the shadow of the tree of life, he would say, "I do not want to stay here." If people were taken to heaven just as they are by nature, without having their hearts regenerated, there would be another rebellion in heaven. Heaven is filled with a company of those who have been twice born.

In John 3:14-15 we read, *As Moses lifted up the serpent in the wilderness, even so must the Son of Man be lifted up; so that whoever believes will in Him have eternal life. Whoever!* – Pay attention to that! Let me tell you who are unsaved what God has done for you. He has done everything that He could do toward your salvation. You do not need to wait for God to do anything more. In one place He asks what more He could have done. *What more was there to do for My vineyard that I have not done in it?* (Isaiah 5:4). He sent His prophets, and they killed them; then He sent His beloved Son, and they murdered Him. Now He has sent the Holy Spirit to convince us of sin and to show us how we are to be saved.

In this chapter we are told how we are to be saved: namely, by Him who was lifted up on the cross. Just as

Moses lifted up the brazen serpent in the wilderness, so must the Son of Man be lifted up, that *whoever believes in Him shall not perish, but have eternal life.* Some people complain and say that it is very unreasonable that they should be held responsible for the sin of a man six thousand years ago. It was not long ago that a man was talking to me about this injustice, as he called it. If a man thinks he is going to answer God in that way, I tell you it will not do him any good. If you are lost, it will not be on account of Adam's sin.

Let me illustrate this, and perhaps you will be better able to understand it. Suppose I am dying of tuberculosis, which I caught from my father or mother. I did not get the disease by any fault of my own or by any neglect of my health; I inherited it, let us suppose. A friend happens to come along; he looks at me and says, "Moody, you are sick. You have tuberculosis."

I reply, "I know it. I do not need anyone to tell me that."

"But," he says, "there is a remedy."

"But, sir, I don't believe it. I have tried the leading physicians in this country and in Europe, and they tell me there is no hope."

"But you know me, Moody; you have known me for years."

"Yes, sir."

"Do you think, then, I would tell you a falsehood?"

"No."

"Well, ten years ago I was as sick as you. I was given up by the physicians to die, but I took this medicine, and it cured me. I am perfectly well. Look at me."

I say, "That is a very unusual case."

"Yes, it may be unusual, but it is a fact. This medicine cured me; take this medicine, and it will cure you. Although it has cost me a great deal, it won't cost you anything. Don't make light of it, I beg of you."

"Well," I say, "I would like to believe you, but this is contrary to my reason."

Hearing this, my friend goes away and returns with another friend who testifies to the same thing. I am still disbelieving, so he goes away and brings another friend, and another, and another, and another; and they all testify to the same thing. They say they were as ill as I was, but they took the same medicine that has been offered to me, and it cured them. My friend then hands me the medicine. I dash it to the ground. I do not believe in its saving power, and I die. The reason is, then, that I rejected the remedy.

> There is no hope for you if you neglect the remedy.

So, if you perish, it will not be because Adam fell, but because you rejected the remedy offered to save you. You will choose darkness rather than light (John 3:19). *How will we escape if we neglect so great a salvation?* (Hebrews 2:3). There is no hope for you if you neglect the remedy. It does no good to look at the wound. If we had been in the Israelite camp and had been bitten by one of the fiery serpents, it would have done us no good to look at the wound. Looking at the wound will never save anyone. What you must do is to look at the remedy – look to Him who has power to save you from your sin.

Behold the camp of the Israelites; look at the scene that is pictured in Numbers 21:6-9! Many are dying because they neglect the remedy that is offered. In that arid desert are many tiny graves; many children have been bitten by the fiery serpents. Fathers and mothers are burying their children. Over there they are just burying a mother; a loved mother is about to be laid in the earth. The family weeps and gathers around the beloved form. You hear the mournful cries; you see the bitter tears. The father is being carried away to his last resting place. There is wailing going up all over the camp. Tears are pouring down for thousands who have passed away; thousands more are dying, and the plague is raging from one end of the camp to the other.

I see in one tent an Israelite mother bending over the form of a beloved boy just coming into the bloom of life, just budding into manhood. She is wiping away the sweat of death that is gathering upon his brow. Soon his eyes are fixed and glassy, for life is ebbing away fast. The mother's heartstrings are torn and bleeding. All at once she hears a noise in the camp. A great shout goes up. What does it mean? She goes to the door of the tent. "What is the noise in the camp?" she asks those passing by.

Someone says, "Why, my good woman, haven't you heard the good news that has come into the camp?"

"No," says the woman. "Good news! What is it?"

"Why, haven't you heard? God has provided a remedy."

"What! For the bitten Israelites? Oh, tell me what the remedy is!"

"Why, God has instructed Moses to make a bronze serpent and to put it on a pole in the middle of the camp. He has declared that whosoever looks upon it shall live. The shout that you hear is the shout of the people when they see the serpent lifted up."

The mother goes back into the tent, and she says, "My boy, I have good news to tell you. You do not need to die! My son, my son, I have come with good news; you can live!" He is astonished but so weak that he cannot walk to the door of the tent. His mother puts her strong arms under him and lifts him up. "Look there; look right there under the hill!"

But the boy does not see anything. He says, "I do not see anything; what is it, Mother?"

She says, "Keep looking, and you will see it." At last he catches a glimpse of the glistening serpent, and behold, he is well!

And so it is with many young converts. Some people say, "Oh, we do not believe in sudden conversions." How long did it take to cure that boy? How long did it take to cure those serpent-bitten Israelites? It was just a look, and they were well.

That Hebrew boy is a young convert. I can imagine that I see him now calling on all who were with him to praise God. He sees another young man bitten as he was, and he runs up to him and tells him, "You do not need to die."

"Oh," the young man replies, "I cannot live; it is not possible. There is not a physician in Israel who can cure me." He does not know that he does not need to die.

"Have you not heard the news? God has provided a remedy."

"What remedy?"

"God has told Moses to lift up a bronze serpent and has said that none of those who look upon that serpent shall die."

I can just imagine the young man. He may be what you call an intellectual man. He says to the young convert, "You do not think I am going to believe anything like that, do you? If the physicians in Israel cannot cure me, how do you think that an old bronze serpent on a pole is going to cure me?"

"Why, sir, I was as sick as you!"

"You do not say so!"

"Yes, I do."

"That is the most astonishing thing I ever heard," says the young man. "I wish you would explain how it works."

"I cannot. I only know that I looked at that serpent, and I was cured. That did it. I just looked; that is all. My mother told me the reports that were being heard through the camp, and I just believed what my mother said, and I am perfectly well."

"Well, I don't believe you were bitten as badly as I have been." The young man pulls up his sleeve. "Look there! That mark shows where I was bitten, and I tell you I was worse than you are."

"Well, if I understood how it works, I would look and get well."

"You do not have to understand it all; simply look and live."

"But, sir, you ask me to do an unreasonable thing. If God had said to take the brass and rub it into the wound, there might be something in the brass that would cure the bite. Young man, explain to me how it works."

I have often seen people before me who have talked in that way. But the young man calls in someone else, takes him into the tent, and says, "Just tell him how the Lord saved you," and he tells the same story; he calls in others, and they all say the same thing.

The young man says it is a very strange thing. "If the Lord had told Moses to go and get some herbs, or roots, and stew them and take the concentrate as a medicine, there would be something in that. But it is so contrary to nature to do such a thing as look at the serpent, that I cannot do it."

"Look and live!"

At length his mother, who has been out in the camp, comes in, and she says, "My boy, I have the best news in the world for you. I was in the camp, and I saw hundreds who were very far gone, and they are all perfectly well now."

The young man says, "I would like to get well; it is a very painful thought to die. I want to go into the promised land, and it is terrible to die here in this wilderness; but the fact is, I do not understand the remedy. It does not appeal to my reason. I cannot believe that I can get well in a moment." And the young man dies because of his own unbelief.

God provided a remedy for this bitten Israelite: "Look and live!" There is eternal life available for every poor sinner. Look, and you can be saved, my reader, this very hour. God has provided a remedy, and it is offered to all. The trouble is that a great many people are looking at the pole. Do not look at the pole; that is the church. You do not need to look at the church; the church is all right, but the church cannot save you. Look beyond the pole. Look at the Crucified One. Look to Calvary. Bear in mind that Jesus died for everyone. You do not need to look at pastors; they are just God's chosen instruments to hold up the Remedy – Christ. And so, my friends, take your eyes off men; take your eyes off the church. Lift your eyes up to Jesus, who took away the sin of the world, and you will find life from this hour.

Thank God, we do not require an education to teach us how to look. That little girl, that little boy, only four years old, who cannot read, can look. When a father is coming home, the mother says to her little boy, "Look! Look! Look!" and the little child learns to look long before he is a year old. That is the way to be saved. It is to look at the *Lamb of God who takes away the sin of the world* (John 1:29). There is life this moment for everyone who is willing to look.

Some people say, "I wish I knew how to be saved." Just take God at His word and trust His Son this very day – this very hour – this very moment. He will save you if you will trust Him. I imagine I hear someone saying, "I do not feel the bite – I do not feel my need for the Savior as much as I wish I did. I know I am a sinner and all that, but I do not feel the bite enough." How much does God want you to feel it?

When I was in Belfast, I knew a doctor who had a friend there, a leading surgeon, and he told me that the surgeon's custom before performing any operation was to say to the patient, "Take a good look at the wound, and then fix your eyes on me; do not take your eyes off me till I get through." I thought at the time that was a good illustration. Sinner, take a good look at your wound, and then fix your eyes on Christ, and do not take them off Him. It is better to look at the Remedy than at the wound. See what a poor wretched sinner you are, and then look at the *Lamb of God who takes away the sin of the world.* Jesus died for the ungodly and the sinner. Say, "I will take Him!" May God help you lift your eyes to the Man on Calvary. As the Israelites looked to the serpent and were healed, so you may look and live.

After the Battle of Pittsburg Landing, I was in a hospital at Murfreesboro. In the middle of the night, I was awakened and told that a man in one of the wards wanted to see me. I went to him and he called me "chaplain" (I was not the chaplain) and said he wanted me to help him be ready to die. I said, "I would take you right up in my arms and carry you into the kingdom of God if I could, but I cannot do it. I cannot help you die!"

And he asked, "Who can?"

I said, "The Lord Jesus Christ can; He came for that purpose."

He shook his head and said, "He cannot save me; I have sinned all my life."

And I said, "But He came to save sinners." I thought of his mother in the north, and I was sure that she was anxious that he should die in peace, so I determined that I would stay with him. I prayed two or three times and repeated all the promises I could, for it was evident that in a few hours he would be gone. I said I wanted to read him a conversation that Christ had with a man who was anxious about his soul. I turned to the third chapter of John. His eyes were riveted on me. When I came to verses 14 and 15, he heard the words, *As Moses lifted up the serpent in the wilderness, even so must the Son of Man be lifted up; so that whoever believes will in Him have eternal life* (John 3:14-15).

He stopped me and said, "Is that written in there?" I said "Yes."

He asked me to read it again, so I did. He leaned his elbows on the cot, clasped his hands together, and said, "That's good; won't you read it again?" I read it the third time and then went on with the rest of the chapter. When I had finished, his eyes were closed, his hands were folded, and there was a smile on his face. Oh, how it was lit up! What change had come over him! I saw his lips quivering, and leaning over him I heard in a faint whisper, *As Moses lifted up the serpent in the wilderness, even so must the Son of Man be lifted up; so that whoever believes will in Him have eternal life.*

He opened his eyes and said, "That's enough; don't read anymore." He lingered a few hours, dwelling on those two verses. Then he went up in one of Christ's chariots to take his seat in the kingdom of God.

Christ said to Nicodemus, *Unless one is born again he cannot see the kingdom of God.* You may see many countries, but there is one country, the land of Beulah, that John Bunyan saw in a vision, that you will never behold unless you are born again, regenerated by Christ. You can look around and see many beautiful trees, but you will never behold the tree of life unless your eyes are made clear by faith in the Savior. You may see the beautiful rivers of the earth, but bear in mind that your eyes will never rest upon the river which bursts out from the throne of God and flows through the kingdom of heaven unless you are born again. God has said it, not man. You will never see the kingdom of God except you are born again. You may see the kings and lords of the earth, but you will never see the King of kings and Lord of lords unless you are born again. When you are in London, you may go to the Tower and see the crown of England, which is worth thousands of dollars and guarded by soldiers, but bear in mind that your eyes will never rest upon the crown of life unless you are born again.

> You will never see the kingdom of God except you are born again.

You may hear the songs of Zion, which are sung here on earth, but one song, the one of Moses and the Lamb, your ears will never hear unless you have been born again; its melody will only delight the ears of those who have been born of the Spirit. You may look upon the beautiful mansions of earth, but keep in mind that you will never see the mansions that Christ has gone to prepare unless you are born again. It is God who says it. You may see ten thousand beautiful things in this world, but you will never see the city that Abraham caught a glimpse of unless you are born again. From that time he became a pilgrim and sojourner (Hebrews 11:8, 10-16). You may often be invited to wedding receptions here, but you will never attend the marriage supper of the Lamb unless you are born again. It is God who says it, dear friend. You may look on the face of your godly mother tonight and know that she is praying for you, but the time will come when you will never see her again unless you are born again.

You may be a young man or a young lady who has recently stood by the bedside of a dying mother, and she may have said, "Be sure to meet me in heaven," and you promised her that you would. But you will never see her again unless you look to the Lamb of God. You should believe Jesus of Nazareth before you believe the unbelievers who say you do not need to be born again.

Parents, if you hope to see your children who have died, you must be born of the Spirit. Possibly you are a father or a mother who has recently laid a loved one in the grave, and your home seems dark and dreary. Never more will you see your child unless you are born again. If you wish to be reunited to your loved one, you must be born again. I may be addressing a father or a mother who has a loved one up there in heaven. If you could hear that loved one's voice, it would say, "Come this way." Have you a godly friend up there?

Young man or young lady, is your dear mother in heaven already? If you could hear her speak, wouldn't she say, "Turn from the world and follow Jesus, my son," "Look to Jesus, my daughter"? If you would ever see her again, you must be born again.

We all have an Elder Brother there. Two thousand

years ago He crossed over, and from the heavenly shores He is calling you to heaven. Let us turn our backs upon the world. Let us give a deaf ear to the world. Let us look to Jesus on the cross and be saved. Then we shall one day see the King in His beauty, and we shall go out no more.

Chapter 3

Two Groups of People

Two men went up into the temple to pray.
(Luke 18:10)

Two groups of people live in our world. The first don't feel their need of a Savior and have not been convicted of sin by the Spirit; the second are convicted of sin and cry, "What must I do to be saved?"

All inquirers can be categorized in one of two groups: either they have the spirit of the Pharisee or they have the spirit of the publican. If a person with the spirit of the Pharisee comes into one of our discussions to ask questions and learn more about being born again, I know of no better Scripture to meet his case than Romans 3:10-11: *As it is written, There is none righteous, not even one; There is none who understands, there is none who seeks for God.*

Attitude of the Pharisee

Paul is speaking here of the natural or unsaved man. *All have turned aside, together they have become useless; There is none who does good, there is not even one* (Romans 3:12). And in Romans 3:17-19: *And the path of peace they have not known. There is no fear of God before their eyes. Now we know that whatever the Law says, it speaks to those who are under the Law, so that every mouth may be closed and all the world may become accountable to God.*

Then observe verses 22 and 23: *For there is no distinction; for all have sinned and fall short of the glory of God.* Not part of the human family – but all – *have sinned and fall short of the glory of God.*

Another verse, which convicts people of their sin is 1 John 1:8: *If we say that we have no sin, we are deceiving ourselves and the truth is not in us.* On one occasion we held meetings in an eastern city of forty thousand inhabitants. A lady came and asked us to pray for her husband, whom she intended to bring into the later meeting. I have traveled a good deal and met many pharisaical men, but this man was so clothed in self-righteousness that you could not get the point of the needle of conviction in anywhere. I said to his wife, "I am glad to see your faith, but we cannot get him to even begin to see God's truth; he is the most self-righteous man I ever saw."

She said, "You must! My heart will break if these meetings end without his conversion." She persisted in bringing him, and I almost got tired of the sight of him. But toward the close of our thirty days of meetings, he came up to me and put his trembling hand on my shoulder.

The place in which the meetings were held was rather cold with an adjoining room where only the gas had been lit. He said to me, "Can't you come in here for a few minutes?" I thought that he was shaking from cold, and I did not particularly wish to go where it was colder. But he said, "I am the worst man in the state of Vermont. I want you to pray for me."

I thought he must have committed a murder or some other awful crime, and I asked, "Is there any one sin that particularly troubles you?"

He answered, "My whole life has been a sin. I have been a conceited, self-righteous Pharisee. I want you to pray for me." He was under deep conviction. Man could not have produced this result, but the Spirit had. About two o'clock in the morning, light broke in upon his soul. He

Unless you repent, you will all likewise perish.
– Luke 13:3

went up and down the business street of the city and told what God had done for him. He has been a most active Christian ever since.

There are four other passages in dealing with inquirers, which were used by Jesus Himself. *Truly, truly, I say to you, unless one is born again he cannot see the kingdom of God* (John 3:3).

In Luke 13:3, we read: *Unless you repent, you will all likewise perish.*

In Matthew 18, when the disciples came to Jesus

to know who was to be the greatest in the kingdom of heaven, He took a little child and set him in the midst and said, *Truly I say to you, unless you are converted and become like children, you will not enter the kingdom of heaven* (Matthew 18:3).

There is another important "unless" in Matthew 5:20: *Unless your righteousness surpasses that of the scribes and Pharisees, you will not enter the kingdom of heaven.*

A person must be made "fit" or ready before he will want to go into the kingdom of God. In considering the story of the Prodigal Son, I would rather go into the kingdom with the younger brother than stay outside with the older who *became angry and was not willing to go in* (Luke 15:28). Heaven would be hell to such a person as this. An older brother who could not rejoice at his younger brother's return would not be fit for the kingdom of God. It is a solemn thing to contemplate, but the curtain drops and leaves him outside with the younger brother inside. To the older brother, the language of the Savior under other circumstances seems appropriate: *Truly I say to you that the tax collectors and prostitutes will get into the kingdom of God before you* (Matthew 21:31).

A lady once came to me and wanted a favor for her daughter. She said, "You must remember I do not agree with you in your doctrine."

I asked, "What is your disagreement?"

She said, "I think your abuse of the older brother is horrible. I think he is a noble character."

I said that I was willing to hear her defend him, but that it was a solemn thing to take up such a position, and the elder brother needed to be converted as much as the younger. When people talk of being moral, it is good to get them to take a good look at the old man pleading with his boy who would not go in.

Attitude of the Publican

But we will move on now to the other group with which we have to deal. It is composed of those who are convinced of sin and from whom the cry comes as from the Philippian jailer, *What must I do to be saved?* (Acts 16:30). To those who utter this penitential cry there is no necessity to administer the law. They already realize that they are sinners. It is good to bring them straight to the Scripture: *Believe in the Lord Jesus, and you will be saved* (Acts 16:31). Many will meet you with a scowl and say, "I don't know what it is to believe," and though the law of heaven declares they must believe in order to be saved, they still ask for something besides that. They want us to tell them what and where and how to believe.

In John 3:35-36 we read: *The Father loves the Son and has given all things into His hand. He who believes in the Son has eternal life; but he who does not obey the Son will not see life, but the wrath of God abides on him.* Now this looks reasonable. Man lost life by unbelief – by not believing God's word; we got life back again by believing – by taking God at His word. In other words, we get up where Adam fell down. He stumbled and fell over the stone of unbelief; we are lifted up and stand upright by believing.

When people say they cannot believe, show them chapter and verse and hold them right to this one thing: "Has God ever broken His promise for these six thousand years?" The devil and men have been trying all the time and have not succeeded in showing that He has broken a single promise. There would be a jubilee in hell today if one word that He has spoken could be broken. If a man says that he cannot believe, it is good to question him on that one thing.

I can believe God better today than I can believe my own heart. *The heart is more deceitful than all else and is desperately sick; Who can understand it?* (Jeremiah 17:9). I can believe God better than I can believe myself. If you want to know the way of life, believe that Jesus Christ is a personal Savior. Put away all doctrines and creeds and come right to the heart of the Son of God. If you have been feeding on dry doctrine, you know there is not much growth on that kind of food. Doctrines are to the soul what the streets that lead to the

You do not get power to love and serve God until you believe.

house of a friend who has invited me to dinner are to the body. They will lead me there if I take the right one, but if I remain in the streets, my hunger will never be satisfied. Feeding on doctrines is like trying to live on dry husks; the soul that doesn't partake of the Bread sent down from heaven will remain lean.

Some ask, "How am I to get my heart warmed?" It

is by believing. You do not get power to love and serve God until you believe.

The apostle John says:

> If we receive the testimony of men, the testi-
> mony of God is greater; for the testimony of
> God is this, that He has testified concerning
> His Son. The one who believes in the Son of
> God has the testimony in himself; the one
> who does not believe God has made Him
> a liar, because he has not believed in the
> testimony that God has given concerning
> His Son. And the testimony is this, that God
> has given us eternal life, and this life is in
> His Son. He who has the Son has the life; he
> who does not have the Son of God does not
> have the life. (1 John 5:9-12)

Human affairs would come to a standstill if we did not listen to the testimony of men. How could we get on in the ordinary affairs of life, and how would business get on, if we disregarded men's testimony? Social and commercial things would come to a standstill within forty-eight hours! This is the drift of the apostle's argument here. *If we receive the testimony of men, the testimony of God is greater.* God has borne witness to Jesus Christ, and if man can believe his fellow men who are frequently telling untruths and whom we are constantly finding unfaithful, why should we not take God at His word and believe His testimony?

Faith is a belief in testimony. It is not a leap in the

dark, as some tell us. That would be no faith at all. God does not ask anyone to believe without giving him something to believe. You might as well ask a man to see without eyes, to hear without ears, and to walk without feet as to ask him to believe without giving him something to believe.

When I started for California, I obtained a guidebook. This told me that after leaving the state of Illinois, I would cross the Mississippi River and then the Missouri. Then I would go into Nebraska, cross the Rocky Mountains to the Mormon settlement at Salt Lake City, and travel by the way of the Sierra Nevada Mountains into San Francisco. I found the guidebook all right as I went along, and I would have been a miserable skeptic if, having proved it to be correct three-fourths of the way, I had said that I would not believe it for the rest of my journey.

Suppose a man, in directing me to the post office, tells me about ten landmarks I would see on the way, and as I headed there, I find nine of them to be as he told me. I would then have good reason to believe that I was near the post office.

If, by believing, I get new life with hope, peace, joy, and rest for my soul that I never had before; if I get self-control and find that I have a power to resist evil and to do good, I have pretty good proof that I am on the right road to *the city which has foundations, whose architect and builder is God* (Hebrews 11:10).

If things have taken place and are now taking place, as recorded in God's Word, I have good reason to conclude that promises and prophecies that remain will be fulfilled. Yet people doubt. There can be no true faith where there is fear. Faith is to take God at His word, unconditionally. There cannot be true peace where there is fear. Perfect love casts out fear (1 John 4:18). How miserable a wife would be if she doubted her husband, and how miserable a mother would feel if, after her boy had gone away from home, she had reason to question her son's devotion only because he rarely contacted her! True love never has a doubt.

There are three things indispensable to faith: knowledge, agreement, and appropriation (personally making use of faith as one's own).

We must know God. *This is eternal life, that they may know You, the only true God, and Jesus Christ whom You have sent* (John 17:3). Then we must not only give our assent to what we know, but we must lay hold of the truth. A person will not be saved by simply giving assent to the plan of salvation; he must also accept Christ as his Savior. He must receive and appropriate Him – take Him as His own – personally trust in Him.

Some people say they cannot tell how a person's life can be affected by what one believes. But let someone cry out that some building in which we happen to be sitting is on fire, and see how quickly we act on our belief and get out. We are influenced by what we believe all the time. We cannot help it. If you believe the record that God has given of Christ, it will quickly affect your whole life.

Consider John 5:24; there is enough truth in that one verse for every soul to rest upon for salvation. It does not leave room for even the shadow of a doubt.

Truly, truly, I say to you, he who hears My word, and believes Him who sent Me, has eternal life, and does not come into judgment, but has passed out of death into life.

Now if a person really hears the word of Jesus, believes with the heart on God (who sent His Son to be the Savior of the world), and lays hold of and appropriates this great salvation, he has no fear of judgment. He will not be looking forward with dread to the great white throne, for we read in 1 John 4:17, *By this, love is perfected with us, so that we may have confidence in the day of judgment; because as He is, so also are we in this world.* If we believe, there is for us no condemnation, no judgment. That is behind us and passed; we will have boldness in the day of judgment.

I remember reading about a man who was on trial for his life. He had friends with influence, and they procured a pardon for him from the king on condition that he was to go through the trial and be condemned. He went into court with the pardon in his pocket. The feeling ran very high against him, and the judge said that the court was shocked that he seemed so unconcerned. But when the sentence was pronounced, the man pulled out the pardon, presented it, and walked out a free man. He had been pardoned, and we have been pardoned too. Let death come, for we have nothing to fear. All the gravediggers in the world cannot dig a grave large enough and deep enough to hold eternal life. All the coffin makers in the world cannot make a coffin large enough and tight enough to hold eternal life. Death had his hand on Christ once, but never again.

Jesus said, *I AM the resurrection and the life; he who*

believes in Me will live even if he dies, and everyone who lives and believes in Me will never die (John 11:25-26). In the book of Revelation we read that the risen Savior said to John, I am *the living One; and I was dead, and behold, I am alive forevermore* (Revelation 1:18). Death cannot touch Him again.

We get life by believing. In fact, we get more than Adam lost, for the redeemed child of God is heir to a richer and more glorious inheritance than Adam in the garden of Eden could ever have conceived, and yes, that inheritance endures forever. It is absolute and cannot be taken away.

I would much rather have my life hidden with Christ in God than lived in the garden of Eden. Even if Adam had been there ten thousand years before he sinned and fell, he still would have had to leave the garden. In Christ Jesus, we are forever secure. The believer is safer than Adam, if these things become real to him. Let us make them a fact and not a fiction. God has said it; that is enough. Let us trust Him even where we cannot see Him. Let the same confidence animate us that was in little Maggie as related in the following simple but touching incident, which I read in the *Bible Treasury*:

> In Christ Jesus, we are forever secure.

I had been absent from home for some days and was wondering, as I again drew near the homestead, if my little Maggie, just old enough to sit up by herself, would remember me. To test her memory, I stationed myself where I could see her, but she could not see me, and I called her name in the familiar tone: "Maggie!" She dropped her playthings, glanced around the room, and then looked down upon her toys. Again I repeated her name: "Maggie!" She once more looked around the room, but not seeing her father's face, she looked very sad and slowly resumed playing with her toys. Once more I called "Maggie!" She dropped her playthings and burst into tears, as she stretched out her arms in the direction from where the sound came. She knew that though she could not see me, I must be there, for she knew my voice.

Now, we have power to see and to hear, and we have power to believe. It is foolish for the doubters to claim that they cannot believe. They can, if they will. But the trouble with most people is that they have connected feeling with believing. Feeling has nothing whatsoever to do with believing. The Bible does not say "he who feels" or "he who feels and believes" has everlasting life. Nothing of the kind. Jesus said, *He who believes has eternal life* (John 6:47). I cannot control my feelings. If I could, I would never feel ill or have a headache or toothache. I would be well all the time. But I can believe God; if we get our feet on that rock, let doubts and fears come and the waves surge around us – the anchor will hold.

Some people are looking at their faith all the time. Faith is the hand that takes the blessing. I heard this illustration of a beggar. Suppose you met a man in the street whom you had known for years to be a beggar. Suppose you offered him some money, and he said to you, "Thank you, but I don't want your money. I am not a beggar."

"How is that?"

"Last night a man put a thousand dollars into my hands."

"He did! How did you know it was good money?"

"I took it to the bank, deposited it, and got a bank book."

"How did you get this gift?"

"I asked for alms, and after the gentleman talked with me, he took out a thousand dollars in cash and put it in my hand."

"How do you know that he put it in the correct hand?"

"What do I care which hand he put the money in, just so I got the money?"

Many people are always wondering whether the faith by which they receive Christ is the right kind, but what is far more essential is to be sure that we have the right kind of Christ.

Faith is the eye of the soul, and who would ever think of taking out an eye to see if it were the right kind as long as the sight was perfect? It is not my taste, but it is what I taste that satisfies my appetite. So, dear friends, it is taking God at His Word that is the means of our salvation. The truth cannot be made too simple.

A man living in the city of New York has a home along the Hudson River. His daughter and her family went to spend the winter with him, and in the course of the season, scarlet fever broke out. One little girl was put in quarantine to be kept separate from the rest. Every morning the old grandfather used to go and tell his grandchild, "Goodbye," before going to his business. On one of these occasions the little thing took the old man by the hand and led him to a corner of the room. Without saying a word, she pointed to the floor where she had arranged some small crackers, which spelled out, "Grandpa, I want a box of paints." He said nothing. On his return home, he hung up his overcoat and went to the room as usual. His little grandchild, without looking to see if her wish had been complied with, took him into the same corner. There he saw, spelled out in the same way, "Grandpa, I thank you for the box of paints." The old man would not have missed pleasing the child for anything. That was faith.

Faith is taking God at His Word, and those people who want some sign are always getting into trouble. God says it; let us believe it.

But some say that faith is the gift of God. So is the air, but you have to breathe it. So is bread, but you have to eat it. So is water, but you have to drink it. Some want a miraculous kind of feeling. That is not faith. *So faith comes from hearing, and hearing by the word of Christ* (Romans 10:17). That is where faith comes from. It is not for me to sit down and wait for faith to come gliding over me with a strange sensation; it is for me to take God at His Word. You cannot believe unless you have something to believe. Take the Word as it is written and appropriate it. Claim it as your own and hold on to it.

In John 6:47-48 we read: *Truly, truly, I say to you, he who believes has eternal life. I am the bread of life.* The bread is close by. Partake of it. I might have thousands of loaves of bread at my home and thousands of hungry people waiting to be given a loaf. They might assent to the fact that the bread was there, but unless they each took a loaf and began eating, their hunger would not be satisfied. So Christ is the bread of heaven, and as the body feeds on natural food, so the soul must feed on Christ.

If a drowning man sees a rope thrown out to rescue him, he must grab hold of it; in order to do so, he must let go of everything else. If a man is sick, he must take the medicine, for simply looking at it will not cure him. A knowledge of Christ will not help the doubter unless he believes in Him and receives Him as his only hope. The bitten Israelites might have believed that the serpent was lifted up, but unless they had looked, they would not have lived (Numbers 21:6-9).

> If a drowning man sees a rope thrown out to rescue him, he must grab hold of it.

I believe that a certain ocean liner will carry me across the ocean, because I have tried it; but this will not help another man who may want to go, unless he acts upon my knowledge. So a knowledge of Christ does not help us unless we act upon it. That is what it is to believe on the Lord Jesus Christ. It is to act on what we believe. Just as someone steps on board a ship to cross the Atlantic, so we must take Christ and make a commitment of our souls to Him. He has promised to keep all safe who put their trust in Him. To believe on the Lord Jesus Christ is simply to take Him at His word.

Chapter 4

Words of Counsel

A bruised reed he will not break.
(Isaiah 42:3; Matthew 12:20)

I t is dangerous for those who are seeking salvation to lean on the experience of other people, and not go on to experience salvation for themselves. Many are waiting for a repetition of the experience of their grandfather or grandmother. I had a friend who was converted in a field, and he thinks the whole town ought to go down into that meadow and be converted. Another was converted under a bridge, and he thinks that if any doubter were to go there, he would find the Lord. The best thing for the anxious is to go right to the Word of God. If there are any people in the world to whom the Word ought to be very precious, they are the ones asking how to be saved.

For instance, a man may say, "I have no strength." Let him turn to Romans 5:6: *For while we were still*

helpless, at the right time Christ died for the ungodly.
It is because we have no strength that we need Christ.
He has come to give strength to the weak.

Another may say, "I cannot see." Christ says, *I AM
the light of the world* (John 8:12). He came not only to
give light, but to *open blind eyes* (Isaiah 42:7).

Another may say, "I do not think a person can be
saved all at once." A person holding that view was in the
consultation room one night, and I drew his attention
to Romans 6:23: *For the wages of sin is death, but the
free gift of God is eternal life in Christ Jesus our Lord.*
How long does it take to accept a gift? There must be
a moment when you do not have it and another when
you have it – a moment when it is another's and the
next when it is yours. It does not take six months to get
eternal life. It may be like the mustard seed however,
very small at the beginning. Some people are converted
so gradually that, like the morning light, it is impossible to tell when the dawn began; while with others,
it is like the flashing of a meteor and the truth bursts
upon them suddenly. I would not go across the street
to prove when I was converted, but what is important
is to know that I really have been.

A child may be so carefully trained that it is impossible to tell when the new birth began, but there must
have been a moment when the change took place and
when he became a partaker of the divine nature.

Some people do not believe in sudden conversion,
but I will challenge anyone to show a conversion in the
New Testament that was not instantaneous. *As Jesus
went on from there, He saw a man called Matthew, sitting*

in the tax collector's booth; and He said to him, Follow Me! And he got up and followed Him (Matthew 9:9). Nothing could be more sudden than that.

Zacchaeus, the publican, sought to see Jesus, and because he was little of stature, he climbed up a tree. *When Jesus came to the place, He looked up and said to him, Zaccheus, hurry and come down* (Luke 19:5). His conversion must have taken place somewhere between the branch and the ground. We are told that he received Jesus joyfully and said, *Behold, Lord, half of my possessions I will give to the poor, and if I have defrauded anyone of anything, I will give back four times as much* (Luke 19:8). Very few in our day could say anything like that in proof of their conversion.

> You will find all through Scripture that conversions were sudden and instantaneous.

The whole house of Cornelius was converted suddenly. Peter preached Christ to him and to those who were with him; the Holy Spirit fell on them, and they were baptized (Acts 10).

On the day of Pentecost, three thousand gladly received the Word. They were not only converted, but they were baptized the same day (Acts 2).

When Philip talked to the eunuch as they went on their way, the eunuch said to Philip, *Look! Water! What prevents me from being baptized?* Philip said, *If you believe with all your heart, you may.* They went down into the water, and the man of great authority under Candace, the queen of the Ethiopians, was baptized and went on his way rejoicing (Acts 8:26-38). You will find all through Scripture that conversions were sudden and instantaneous.

Suppose a man has been in the habit of stealing money from his employer. If he has taken $1,000 this year, should we tell him to take only $500 the next year and less the next year and the next, until in five years the sum taken would be only $50? That approach would be based on the same principle as gradual conversion.

If such a person were brought before the court and pardoned because he could not change his life of crime all at once, it would be considered a very strange proceeding.

The Bible says, *He who steals must steal no longer* (Ephesians 4:28). It is an about-face, a complete reversal in direction! Suppose a person is in the habit of cursing one hundred times a day. Should we advise him not to swear more than ninety times the following day and eighty the next day, so that in time he would get rid of the habit? The Savior says, *Make no oath at all* (Matthew 5:34).

Suppose another man is in the habit of getting drunk and beating his wife twice a month; if he only beat her once a month and then only once every six months, that would be as reasonable as gradual conversion. Suppose Ananias had been sent to Paul who was on his way to Damascus, breathing out threats to slaughter the disciples and cast them into prison. Would Ananias tell him not to kill as many as he intended or to let hatred die out of his heart gradually but not all at once? Suppose Paul had been told not to stop breathing out threats to slaughter or not to preach Christ immediately, because the philosophers would say that the change was so sudden, it would not hold out. This would be the same kind of reasoning used by those who do not believe in instantaneous conversion.

Then another group will say that they are afraid that new believers will not stand firm – that they might fall away from Jesus. This group is numerous and very hopeful. I like to see a man distrust himself. It is a good thing for these people to look to God and to remember that he does not hold God, but God holds him. Some want to receive Christ, but the important thing is for Christ to receive you in answer to prayer. Let people in this situation read Psalm 121:

> I will lift up my eyes to the mountains;
> From where shall my help come? .
>
> My help comes from the LORD, Who made heaven and earth.
>
> He will not allow your foot to slip; He who keeps you will not slumber.
>
> Behold, He who keeps Israel will neither slumber nor sleep.
>
> The LORD is your keeper; The LORD is your shade on your right hand.
>
> The sun will not smite you by day, nor the moon by night.
>
> The LORD will protect you from all evil; He will keep your soul.
>
> The LORD will guard your going out and your coming in from this time forth and forever.

Someone called that the traveler's psalm. It is a beautiful psalm for those of us who are pilgrims through this world, and it is a psalm with which we should be well acquainted.

God can do what He has done before. He kept Joseph in Egypt, Moses before Pharaoh, Daniel in Babylon, and He enabled Elijah to stand before Ahab in that dark day. I am so thankful that these were men *with a nature like ours* (James 5:17). It was God who made them so great. What we need to do is to look to God. True faith is man's weakness leaning on God's strength. When man has no strength, he can lean on God and become powerful. The trouble is that we have too much strength and confidence in ourselves.

Hebrews 6:17-20 tells a similar message:

> *In the same way God, desiring even more to show to the heirs of the promise the unchangeableness of His purpose, interposed with an oath, so that by two unchangeable things in which it is impossible for God to lie, we who have taken refuge would have strong encouragement to take hold of the hope set before us. This hope we have as an anchor of the soul, a hope both sure and steadfast and one which enters within the veil, where Jesus has entered as a forerunner for us, having become a high priest forever according to the order of Melchizedek.*

These are precious verses to those who are afraid of falling, who fear that they will not hold out. It is God's work to hold. It is the shepherd's business to keep the sheep. Who ever heard of the sheep going to bring back the shepherd? People have the idea that they have to keep themselves and Christ, too. This is a false idea. The work of the Good Shepherd is to look after His sheep and to take care of those who trust Him.

> It is the shepherd's business to keep the sheep.

He has promised to do it. I once heard that when a sea captain was dying, he said, "Glory to God; the anchor holds." He trusted in Christ. His anchor had taken hold of the solid rock. An Irishman said on one occasion that he trembled, but the Rock never did. We want to get sure footing.

In 2 Timothy 1:12 Paul says, *I know whom I have believed and I am convinced that He is able to guard what I have entrusted to Him until that day.* That was Paul's persuasion.

During the late war of the rebellion, as one of the chaplains was going through the hospitals, he came to a man who was dying. Finding that he was a Christian, the chaplain asked to what persuasion or religious group he belonged, and he was told "Paul's persuasion."

"Is he a Methodist?" the chaplain asked, for the Methodists all claim Paul.

"No."

"Is he a Presbyterian?" for the Presbyterians lay special claim to Paul.

"No," was the answer.

"Does he belong to the Episcopal Church?" for all the Episcopalian brethren contend that they have a claim to the chief apostle.

"No," he was not an Episcopalian.

"Then, to what persuasion does he belong?"

"*I . . . am convinced that He is able to guard what I have entrusted to Him until that day.*" It is a grand persuasion, and it gave the dying soldier rest in a dying hour.

Let those who fear that they will not hold out turn to the 24th verse of the epistle of Jude: *Now to Him who is able to keep you from stumbling, and to make you stand in the presence of His glory blameless with great joy.*

Then look at Isaiah 41:10: *Do not fear, for I am with you; Do not anxiously look about you, for I am your God. I will strengthen you, surely I will help you, surely I will uphold you with My righteous right hand.*

Then see verse 13: *For I am the LORD your God, who upholds your right hand, who says to you, Do not fear, I will help you.*

Now if God has my right hand in His, can't He hold me and keep me? Doesn't God have the power to keep? The great God who made heaven and earth can keep a poor sinner like you and like me if we trust Him. To refrain from being confident in God for fear of falling would be like a man who refused a pardon for fear that he would go to prison again or like a drowning man who refused to be rescued because he was afraid of falling into the water again.

Many people look at the Christian life and fear that they will not have enough strength to hold out to the end. They forget the promise that *according to your days, so will your leisurely walk be* (Deuteronomy 33:25). It reminds me of the pendulum of the clock that grew disheartened at the thought of having to travel so many thousands of miles, but when it reflected that the distance was to be accomplished by "tick, tick, tick," it took fresh courage to continue its daily journey. So it is the special privilege of the Christian to commit himself to the keeping of his heavenly Father and to trust Him day by day. It is a comforting thing to know that the Lord will not begin the good work without also finishing it (Philippians 1:6).

There are two types of skeptics. One type has honest difficulties and looks for answers; the other type delights only in discussion but does not want to listen or reason. I used to think that this latter type would always be a thorn in my flesh, but they do not bother me now. I now expect to find them right along the journey. Men of this character used to hang around Christ to entangle Him in His talk. They come into our meetings to hold a discussion. To them I recommend Paul's advice to Timothy: *But refuse foolish and ignorant speculations, knowing that they produce quarrels* (2 Timothy 2:23). Many young converts make a big mistake by thinking that they are to defend the whole Bible. I knew very little of the Bible when I was first converted, and I thought that I had to defend it from beginning to end against all who came, but a Boston skeptic confronted me, floored all my arguments at

> It is the special privilege of the Christian to commit himself to the keeping of his heavenly Father and to trust Him day by day.

once, and discouraged me. I have recovered from that now. I do not profess to understand many things in the Word of God.

When I am asked what I do with them, I say, "I don't do anything."

"How do you explain them?"

"I don't explain them."

"What do you do with them?"

"Why, I believe them."

And when I am told, "I would not believe anything that I do not understand," I simply reply that I do.

There are many things, which were dark and mysterious to me five years ago, on which I have since been enlightened. I expect to discover new things about God throughout eternity. I make a point of not discussing disputed passages of Scripture. An old preacher has said that some people, if they want to eat fish, begin by picking the bones. As for me, I leave such things until I can see them clearly. I am not obligated to explain what I do not comprehend. *The secret things belong to the LORD our God, but the things revealed belong to us and to our sons forever* (Deuteronomy 29:29). I take these and eat and feed upon them in order to get spiritual strength.

There is sound advice in Titus 3:9: *But avoid foolish controversies and genealogies and strife and disputes about the Law, for they are unprofitable and worthless.*

If I meet an honest skeptic, I deal as tenderly with him as a mother would deal with her sick child. I have no sympathy with those people who, because a man is skeptical, cast him off and will have nothing to do with him.

I was in a consultation some time ago, and I took a skeptic to a Christian lady whom I had known some time, thinking that she would deal well with the skeptic. On looking around soon after, I noticed the inquirer leaving the hall. I asked, "Why did you let her go?"

"Oh, she is a skeptic!" was the reply. I ran to the door and stopped her. I introduced her to another Christian worker who spent over an hour with her in conversation and prayer. He visited her and her husband, and in the course of a week, that intelligent lady cast off her skepticism and became an active Christian. It took time, tact, and prayer, but if this person is honest, we ought to deal with such a one as the Master would have dealt with us.

Here are a few passages for doubting inquirers: *If anyone is willing to do His will, he will know of the teaching, whether it is of God or whether I speak from Myself* (John 7:17). If a man is not willing to do the will of God, he will not know the doctrine. There are no skeptics who are ignorant of the fact that God desires them to give up sin. If a person is willing to turn from sin and take the light and thank God for what He does give, not expecting to fully understand the whole Bible all at once, he will get more light day by day, make progress step by step, and be led right out of darkness and into the clear light of heaven.

In Daniel 12:10 we are told: *Many will be purged, purified and refined, but the wicked will act wickedly; and none of the wicked will understand, but those who have insight will understand.* God will never reveal His secrets to His enemies. Never! And if a man persists in living in sin, he will not know the doctrines of God.

The secret of the LORD is for those who fear Him, and He will make them know His covenant (Psalm 25:14). In John 15:15 we read: *No longer do I call you slaves, for the slave does not know what his master is doing; but I have called you friends, for all things that I have heard from My Father I have made known to you.* When you become friends of Christ, you will know His secrets. *The LORD said, Shall I hide from Abraham what I am about to do?* (Genesis 18:17).

Those who resemble God are the most likely to understand God. If a person is not willing to turn from sin, he will not know God's will, nor will God reveal His secrets to him. But if a man is willing to turn from sin, he will be surprised to see how the light will come in!

> If a person is not willing to turn from sin, he will not know God's will, nor will God reveal His secrets to him.

I remember one night when the Bible was the driest and darkest book in the universe to me. The next day it became entirely different. I thought I had the key to it. I had been born of the Spirit. But before I knew anything of the mind of God, I had to give up my sin. I believe God meets every soul on the spot of self-surrender, when they are willing to let Him guide and lead. The trouble with many skeptics is their conceit. They think they know more than the Almighty, and they do not come in a teachable spirit.

But the moment a person comes in a receptive spirit, he is blessed. *But if any of you lacks wisdom, let him ask of God, who gives to all generously and without reproach, and it will be given to him* (James 1:5).

Chapter 5

A Divine Savior

*You are the Christ, the Son of the living
God.* (Matthew 16:16; John 6:69)

One group of doubters does not believe in the
divinity of Christ. Many passages shed light on
this subject. In 1 Corinthians 15:47 we are told, *The
first man is from the earth, earthy; the second man is
from heaven.*

First John 5:20 says, *And we know that the Son of
God has come, and has given us understanding so that
we may know Him who is true; and we are in Him who
is true, in His Son Jesus Christ. This is the true God
and eternal life.*

Read John 17:3: *This is eternal life, that they may
know You, the only true God, and Jesus Christ whom
You have sent.*

Then consider Mark 14:60-64:

*The high priest stood up and came for-
ward and questioned Jesus, saying, Do You
not answer? What is it that these men are
testifying against You? But He kept silent
and did not answer. Again the high priest
was questioning Him, and saying to Him,
Are You the Christ, the Son of the Blessed
One? And Jesus said, I AM; and you shall
see the Son of Man sitting at the right hand
of power, and coming with the clouds of
heaven. Tearing his clothes, the high priest
said, What further need do we have of
witnesses? You have heard the blasphemy;
how does it seem to you? And they all condemned Him to be deserving of death.*

What brought me to believe in the divinity of Christ
was this: I did not know how to categorize or describe
Christ or what to do with Him, if He were not divine.
When I was a boy, I thought that He was a good man
like Moses, Joseph, or Abraham. I even thought that
He was the best man who had ever lived on the earth.
But I found that Christ had a higher claim. He claimed
to be man and one with God, to be divine, and to have
come from heaven. He said, *Before Abraham was born,
I AM* (John 8:58). I could not understand this, and I was
driven to the conclusion – and I challenge any honest
person to deny the inference or meet the argument – that
Jesus Christ is either an impostor or deceiver, or He is
the God-Man – God manifest in the flesh.

Here are some reasons why this must be so. The first

commandment is *You shall have no other gods before Me* (Exodus 20:3). Look at the millions throughout Christendom who worship Jesus Christ as God. If Jesus is not God, this is idolatry. We would all be guilty of breaking the first commandment if Jesus Christ were just a man, a created being, and not what He claims to be.

Some people who do not admit His divinity say that He was the best man who ever lived; but if He were not divine, He should not be considered a good man, because He claimed an honor and dignity to which these very people declare He had no right or title. That would classify Him as a deceiver.

Others say that He thought He was divine but that He was deceived, as if Jesus Christ were carried away by a delusion and deception and thought that He was more than He was! I could not conceive of a lower opinion of Jesus Christ than that. This would not only make Him out to be an impostor but also indicate He was out of His mind and did not know who He was or where He came from. Now if Jesus Christ was not what He claimed to be – the Savior of the world – and if He did not come from heaven, He was a blatant deceiver.

> How can anyone read the life of Jesus Christ and make Him out to be a deceiver?

But how can anyone read the life of Jesus Christ and make Him out to be a deceiver? A man generally has some motive for being an impostor. What was Christ's motive? He knew that the course He was on would take Him to the cross, that His name would be cast out as vile, and that many of His followers would be called upon to lay down their lives for His sake. Nearly every one of the apostles became martyrs, and they were considered as garbage in the midst of the people. If a man is an impostor, he has a motive behind his hypocrisy. But what was Christ's motive? The record is that He *went about doing good* (Acts 10:38). This is not the work of an impostor. Don't let the enemy of your soul deceive you.

In John 5:21-23 we read:

> *For just as the Father raises the dead and gives them life, even so the Son also gives life to whom He wishes. For not even the Father judges anyone, but He has given all judgment to the Son, so that all will honor the Son even as they honor the Father. He who does not honor the Son does not honor the Father who sent Him.*

According to the Jewish law, if a man were a blasphemer, he was to be put to death; if Jesus Christ was only a mere human, then it is clearly blasphemy to say, *He who does not honor the Son does not honor the Father who sent Him.* That is downright blasphemy if Christ is not divine. If Moses or Elijah or Elisha or any other mortal had said, "You must honor me as you honor God" and had put himself on a level with God, it would have been absolute blasphemy.

The Jews put Christ to death because they said that He was not what He claimed to be. It was on that testimony He was put under oath. The high priest said, *I adjure You by the living God, that You tell us whether You are the Christ, the Son of God* (Matthew 26:63). *The Jews then gathered around Him, and were saying to Him, How long will You keep us in suspense? If You are the Christ, tell us plainly.* Jesus said, *I and the Father are one. The Jews picked up stones again to stone Him* (John 10:24, 30-31). They said they did not want to hear more, for that was blasphemy. It was for declaring Himself to be the Son of God that Jesus was condemned and put to death (Matthew 26:63-66).

Now if Jesus Christ were just a mere man, then the Jews did right according to their law by putting Him to death. In Leviticus 24:16 we read, *Moreover, the one who blasphemes the name of the LORD shall surely be put to death; all the congregation shall certainly stone him. The alien as well as the native, when he blasphemes the Name, shall be put to death.* This law obligated them to put to death everyone who blasphemed. It was making the statement that He was divine that cost Jesus His life, and according to the Mosaic Law, He ought to have suffered the death penalty. In John 16:15 Jesus says, *All things that the Father has are Mine; therefore I said that He takes of Mine and will disclose it to you.* How could He be just a good man and use language like that? No doubt has ever entered my mind on that point, since I was converted. A notorious sinner was once asked how he could prove the divinity of Christ. His answer was, "Why, He has saved me; that is a pretty good proof, is it not?"

An unbeliever on one occasion said to me, "I have been studying the life of John the Baptist, Mr. Moody.

Why don't you preach more about him? He was a greater character than Christ. You would do a greater work."

I said to him, "My friend, you preach John the Baptist, and I will follow you and preach Christ, and we will see who will do the most good."

"You will do the most good," he said, "because the people are so superstitious."

Ah! John was beheaded, and his disciples begged for his body and buried it, but Christ has risen from the dead. He has *ascended on high, You have led captive Your captives; You have received gifts among men* (Psalm 68:18). Our Christ lives. Many people have not found out that Christ has risen from the grave. They worship a dead Savior. They are like Mary, who said, *They have taken away my Lord, and I do not know where they have laid Him* (John 20:13). That is the trouble with those who doubt the divinity of our Lord.

Then look at Matthew 18:20: *For where two or three have gathered together in My name, I am there in their midst.* Well now, if Jesus is just a man, how can He be there? All these are strong passages. Again in Matthew 28:18: *And Jesus came up and spoke to them, saying, All authority has been given to Me in heaven and on earth.* Could He be a mere man and talk in that way? *All authority has been given to Me in heaven and on earth.* Read Matthew 28:20: *Teaching them to observe all that I commanded you; and lo, I am with you always, even to the end of the age.* If He were just a man, how could He be with us? Yet He says, *I am with you always, even to the end of the age.*

Now look at Mark 2:7-9:

> *Why does this man speak that way? He is*
> *blaspheming; who can forgive sins but God*
> *alone? Immediately Jesus, aware in His*
> *spirit that they were reasoning that way*
> *within themselves, said to them, Why are*
> *you reasoning about these things in your*
> *hearts? Which is easier, to say to the para-*
> *lytic, Your sins are forgiven; or to say, Get*
> *up, and pick up your pallet and walk?*

Some men will meet you and say, "Didn't Elisha also raise the dead?" Notice that in the rare instances in which men have raised the dead, they did it by the power of God. They called on God to do it. But when Christ was on earth, He did not need to call upon the Father to bring the dead to life. When He went to the house of Jairus, He said, *Little girl, I say to you, get up* (Mark 5:41).

He had power to impart life. When they were carrying the young man out of Nain, Jesus had compassion on the widowed mother and came and touched the casket and said, *Young man, I say to you, arise* (Luke 7:14). He spoke, and the dead arose. When He raised Lazarus, He called with a loud voice, *Lazarus, come forth* (John 11:43). Lazarus heard and came forth. Someone has said that it was a good thing that Lazarus was mentioned by name, or all the dead within the sound of Christ's voice would immediately have risen.

In John 5:25, Jesus says, *Truly, truly, I say to you, an hour is coming and now is, when the dead will hear the voice of the Son of God, and those who hear will live.*

What blasphemy this would have been, if He had not been divine! The proof is overwhelming, if you only examine the Word of God.

And then another thing – no good man except Jesus Christ has ever allowed anybody to worship him. When this was done, Jesus never rebuked the worshiper. In John 9:38 we read that when the blind man was found by Christ, he said, *Lord, I believe. And he worshiped Him.* The Lord did not rebuke him.

Revelation 22:6-9 says:

> *And he said to me, These words are faithful and true; and the Lord, the God of the spirits of the prophets, sent His angel to show to His bond-servants the things which must soon take place. And behold, I am coming quickly. Blessed is he who heeds the words of the prophecy of this book. I, John, am the one who heard and saw these things. And when I heard and saw, I fell down to worship at the feet of the angel who showed me these things. But he said to me, Do not do that. I am a fellow servant of yours and of your brethren the prophets and of those who heed the words of this book. Worship God.*

We see here that even that angel would not allow John to worship him. Even an angel from heaven! And if Gabriel came down here from the presence of God, it would be a sin to worship him or any seraph or any cherub, or Michael or any archangel. *Worship God!* If

Jesus Christ were not God manifest in the flesh, we are guilty of idolatry in worshiping Him. In Matthew 14:33 we read: *And those who were in the boat worshiped Him, saying, You are certainly God's Son!* He did not rebuke them. In Matthew 8:2 we read: *And a leper came to Him and bowed down before Him, and said, Lord, if You are willing, You can make me clean.* See Matthew 15:25: *But she came and began to bow down before Him, saying, Lord, help me!*

> Let us rest on His all-atoning work and go forth to serve Him all the days of our lives.

There are many other passages, but I give these as sufficient in my opinion to prove the divinity of our Lord beyond any doubt.

In Acts 14 we are told that the heathen at Lystra came with garlands and would have offered sacrifice to Paul and Barnabas because they had cured a lame man, but the evangelists rent their clothes and told these Lystrans that they were only men and were not to be worshipped, as if it were a great sin. If Jesus Christ is a mere man, we are all guilty of a great sin in worshipping Him.

But if He is, as we believe, the only-begotten and well-beloved Son of God, let us yield to His claims upon us. Let us rest on His all-atoning work and go forth to serve Him all the days of our lives.

Chapter 6

Repentance and Restitution

God is now declaring to men that all people everywhere should repent. (Acts 17:30)

Repentance is one of the fundamental doctrines of the Bible, but I believe it is one of those truths that many people do not understand very well today. More people today are in the mist and darkness about repentance, regeneration, the atonement, and similar basic truths than about any other doctrines, Even though we have heard about them from our earliest years. If I were to ask for a definition of repentance, many would give a strange and false explanation of it.

A person is not prepared to believe or to receive the gospel unless he is ready to repent of his sins and turn from them. Until John the Baptist met Christ, he had but one text: *Repent, for the kingdom of heaven is at hand* (Matthew 3:2). But if he had continued to say this and had stopped there without pointing the people to Christ, the Lamb of God, he would not have accomplished much.

When Christ came, He took up the same wilderness cry: *Repent, for the kingdom of heaven is at hand* (Matthew 4:17). When our Lord sent out His disciples, it was with the same message – *that men should repent* (Mark 6:12). After Jesus had been glorified and when the Holy Spirit came down, Peter raised the same cry on the day of Pentecost: *Repent*. It was this preaching – repent and believe the gospel – that brought about such marvelous results (Acts 2:38-47). When Paul went to Athens, he uttered the same cry: God *is now declaring to men that all people everywhere should repent* (Acts 17:30).

Before I speak of what repentance is, let me briefly say what it is not.

Repentance is not fear. Many people have confused the two. They think they have to be alarmed and terrified, and they wait for some kind of fear to come down upon them. Multitudes become alarmed but do not really repent. Sometimes during a terrible storm, men at sea, who had been very profane, suddenly grow quiet and cry to God for mercy when danger comes. But you would not say they repented, because when the storm passes, they go on swearing the same as before. You might think that the king of Egypt repented when God sent the terrible plagues upon him and his land, but it was not repentance at all. The moment God's hand was removed, Pharaoh's heart was harder than ever. He did not turn from a single sin; he was the same man. There was no true repentance there.

Often when death comes into a family, it looks as if the event would result in the conversion of all who are in the house, but within six months, all may be forgotten. Some who read this have possibly passed through that experience. When God's hand was heavy upon them, it looked as if they were going to repent, but when the trial was removed, the impression was gone.

Repentance is not feeling. Many people wait for a certain kind of feeling to come. They would like to turn to God but think they cannot do it until this feeling comes. When I was in Baltimore, I preached every Sunday in the penitentiary to nine hundred convicts. There was hardly a man there who did not feel miserable enough; they had plenty of feeling. For the first week or ten days of their imprisonment, many of them cried half the time. But when they were released, most of them went right back to their old ways. The truth was that they felt very bad because they got caught; that was all. You have seen someone during a time of difficulty show a good deal of feeling, but very often it is only because he got into trouble – not because he cares that he has committed sin or because his conscience tells him he has done evil in the sight of God. It seems as if the trial would result in true repentance, but the feeling too often passes away.

Repentance is not fasting and afflicting the body. A person may fast for weeks and months and years but not repent of one sin.

Repentance is not remorse. Judas had terrible remorse – enough to make him go and hang himself – but that was not repentance. I believe that if he had gone to his Lord, fallen on his face, and confessed his sin, he might have been forgiven. Instead of this, he went to the priests and then put an end to his life. A man may do all sorts of penance, but there is no true repentance in that. Remember that. You cannot meet the claims of God by offering the fruit of your body for the sin of your soul. Away with such a delusion!

Repentance is not conviction of sin. That may sound strange to some. I have seen people under such deep conviction of sin that they could not sleep at night. They could not enjoy a single meal. They went on for months in this state, and yet they were not converted. They did not truly repent. Do not confuse conviction of sin with repentance.

Repentance is not praying. That, too, may sound strange. Many people, when they become anxious about their soul's salvation, say, "I will pray and read the Bible." They think that will bring about the desired effect, but it will not do it. You may read the Bible and cry to God a great deal and yet never repent. Many people cry loudly to God but do not repent.

Repentance is not refraining from some sin. A

great many people make that mistake. A man who has been a drunkard might make a promise to stop drinking. Refraining from one sin is not repentance. Forsaking one vice is like breaking off one limb of a tree when the whole tree has to come down. A profane man stops swearing; that is very good. But if he does not turn from every sin, it is not repentance; it is not the work of God in the soul. When God works, He cuts down the whole tree. He wants to have you turn from every sin.

Suppose I am in a ship out at sea, and I find that the ship leaks in three or four places. I may go and stop up one hole, but the vessel will still sink. Or suppose I am wounded in three or four places, and I get a remedy for one wound; if the other two or three wounds are neglected, my life will soon be gone. True repentance is not merely turning from this or that particular sin.

Well then, what is repentance? I will give you a good definition: it is "right-about-face or complete reversal!" In the Irish language, the word *repentance* means even more than "right-about-face!" It implies that a man who has been walking in one direction has not only turned around but is actually walking in exactly the opposite direction. *Turn back, turn back from your evil ways! Why then will you die?* (Ezekiel 33:11). A man may have little feeling or much feeling, but if he does not turn away from sin, God will not have mercy on him.

Repentance has also been described as a change of mind. For instance, Christ told this parable: *A man had two sons, and he came to the first and said, Son, go work today in the vineyard. And he answered, I will not*. After he had said *I will not*, he thought it over and changed his mind. *But afterward he regretted it and went* (Matthew 21:28-29). Perhaps he may have said to himself, "I did not speak very respectfully to my father. He asked me to go and work, and I told him I would not go. I think I was wrong."

> Man is born with his face turned away from God.

But suppose he had only said this and still had not gone; that would not be repentance. But he did go. He was not only convinced that he was wrong, but he went off into the vineyard and worked. That is Christ's definition of repentance. If a man says, "By the grace of God I will forsake my sin and do His will," that is repentance – a complete change in direction.

Someone has said that man is born with his face turned away from God. When he truly repents, he is turned around towards God; he leaves his old life.

Can a person repent at once? Certainly he can. It does not take long to turn around. It does not take a man six months to change his mind. A ship went down some time ago on the Newfoundland coast. As it was bearing towards the shore, the captain could have given orders to reverse the engines and turn back. If the engines had been reversed at that moment, the ship would have been saved. But there was a moment when it was too late. So there is a moment, I believe, in every person's life when he can stop and say, "By the grace of God I will go no further towards death and ruin. I repent of my sins and turn from them." You may say you don't have enough feeling, but if you are convinced that you are on the wrong road, turn around and say, "I will no longer go in the way of rebellion and sin as I have done."

Just then, when you are willing to turn toward God, salvation may be yours. I find that every case of conversion recorded in the Bible was instantaneous. Repentance and faith came suddenly. The moment a man made up his mind, God gave him the power. God does not ask anyone to do what he is not able to do. He would not command *all people everywhere should repent* if they were not able to do so (Acts 17:30). You have no one to blame but yourself if you do not repent and believe the gospel.

One of the leading ministers of the gospel in Ohio wrote me a letter some time ago, describing his conversion. It forcibly illustrates this point of instantaneous decision. He wrote:

> I was nineteen years old and was reading law with a Christian lawyer in Vermont. One afternoon when he was away from home, his good wife said to me, as I came into the house, "I want you to go to class with me tonight and become a Christian so you can conduct family worship here while my husband is away."
>
> "Well, I'll do it," I said, without any thought. When I came into the house again, she asked me if I was honest in what I had said. I replied, "Yes, so far as going to the

meeting with you is concerned; that is only courteous."

I went with her to the class, as I had often done before. About a dozen people were present in a little schoolhouse. The leader had spoken to everyone in the room except me and two others. He was speaking to the person next to me, when the thought occurred to me, *He will ask me if I have anything to say.* I said to myself, *I have decided to be a Christian sometime; why not begin now?*

In less time than a minute after these thoughts had passed through my mind, he said, speaking to me familiarly – for he knew me very well – "Brother Charles, have you anything to say?"

I replied with perfect coolness, "Yes, sir. I have just decided in the last thirty seconds that I will begin a Christian life, and I would like to have you pray for me."

My coolness staggered him. I think he almost doubted my sincerity. He said very little, but passed on and spoke to the other two. After a few general remarks, he turned to me and said, "Brother Charles, will you close the meeting with prayer?"

He knew I had never prayed in public. Up to this moment I had no feeling. This was purely a business transaction. My first thought was that I cannot pray, and I will ask him to excuse me. My second thought was that I have said I will begin a Christian life, and this is a part of it. So I said, "Let us pray." And somewhere between the time I started to kneel and the time my knees struck the floor, the Lord converted my soul.

The first words I said were, "Glory to God!" What I said after that I do not know, and it does not matter, for my soul was too full to say much but "Glory!" From that hour on, the devil has never dared to challenge my conversion. To Christ be all the praise.

Many people are waiting for some sort of miraculous feeling to come over them – some mysterious kind of faith. I was speaking to a man some years ago, and he always had the same answer to give me. For five years I tried to win him to Christ, and every year he said, "It hasn't struck me yet."

"Man, what do you mean? What hasn't struck you?"

"Well," he said, "I am not going to become a Christian until it strikes me, and it has not struck me yet. I do not see it in the way you see it."

"But don't you know you are a sinner?"

"Yes, I know I am a sinner."

"Well, don't you know that God wants to have mercy

on you – that there is forgiveness with God? He wants you to repent and come to Him."

"Yes, I know that; but it hasn't struck me yet."

He always fell back on that. Poor man! He went down to his grave in a state of indecision. Sixty long years God gave him to repent, and all he had to say at the end of those years was that it hadn't struck him yet.

Is any reader waiting for some strange feeling? Nowhere in the Bible is a person told to wait. God is commanding you now to repent.

Do you think God can forgive someone when he does not want to be forgiven? Would he be happy if God forgave him in this state of mind? If your boy has done wrong and will not repent, you cannot forgive him. You would be doing him an injustice. Suppose he goes to your desk, steals ten dollars, and squanders it. When you come home, your spouse tells you what your boy has done. You ask if it is true, and he denies it, but at last you have certain proof. Even when he finds he cannot deny it any longer, he will not confess the sin but says he will do it again the first chance he gets.

God is commanding you now to repent.

Would you say to him, "Well, I forgive you," and leave the matter there? No, there are real consequences for everything we do, both here on earth and at the judgment! Yet people say that God is going to save everyone, whether they repent or not – drunkards, thieves, harlots, whoremongers, it makes no difference.

"God is so merciful," they say. Dear friend, do not be deceived by the god of this world. Where there is true repentance and a turning from sin unto God, He will meet and bless you, but He never blesses until there is sincere repentance.

David made a woeful mistake in this respect with his rebellious son Absalom. He could not have done his son a greater injustice than to forgive him when his heart was unchanged. There could be no true reconciliation between them when there was no repentance. But God does not make these mistakes. David got into trouble because of his error of judgment. His son soon drove his father from the throne.

Speaking on repentance, Dr. Brooks of St. Louis remarks:

> Repentance, strictly speaking, means a change of mind or purpose; consequently, it is the judgment, which the sinner pronounces upon himself in view of the love of God displayed in the death of Christ, connected with the abandonment of all confidence in himself and with trust in the only Savior of sinners. Saving repentance and saving faith always go together, and you don't need to be worried about repentance if you will believe.

Some people are not sure that they have repented enough. If you mean by this that you must repent in order to incline God to be merciful to you, the sooner you give over such repentance, the better. God is already merciful, as He has fully shown at the cross of Calvary. It is a grievous dishonor to His heart of love if you think that your tears and anguish will move Him, not knowing that *the kindness of God leads you to repentance* (Romans 2:4). It is not your badness, therefore, but His goodness that leads to repentance; therefore, the true way to repent is to believe on the Lord Jesus Christ, *who was delivered over because of our transgressions, and was raised because of our justification* (Romans 4:25).

If there is true repentance, it will bring forth fruit. If we have done wrong to anyone, we should never ask God to forgive us until we are willing to make restitution to the person we have wronged. If I have done any person a great injustice and can make it good, I don't need to ask God to forgive me until I am willing to make it good. Suppose I have taken something that does not belong to me. I have no right to expect forgiveness until I make restitution.

I remember preaching in one of our large cities when a fine-looking man came up to me after the sermon. He was in great distress of mind. "The fact is," he said, "I am an embezzler. I have taken money that belonged to my employers. How can I become a Christian without restoring it?"

I asked him, "Have you got the money?"

He told me he did not have it all. He had taken about $1,500, and he still had about $900. He said, "Couldn't I take that money and start a business to make enough to pay them back?"

I told him that was a delusion of Satan, and he could not expect to prosper on stolen money. I told him that he should restore all the money that was left and ask his employers to have mercy on him and forgive him.

"But they will put me in prison," he said. "Can't you give me any help?"

"No, you must restore the money before you can expect to get any help from God."

"It is pretty hard," he said.

"Yes. it is hard, but the great mistake was in doing the wrong in the first place."

His burden became so heavy that it became unbearable. He handed me the money – about $950 – and asked me to take it back to his employers. The next evening the two employers met with me in a side room of the church. I laid the money down and informed them it was from one of their employees. I told them the story and said he wanted mercy from them, not justice. The tears trickled down the cheeks of these two men, and they said, "Forgive him! Yes, we will be glad to forgive him." I went down stairs and brought him up. After he had confessed his guilt and had been forgiven, we all got down on our knees and had a blessed prayer meeting. God met us and blessed us there.

Some time ago a friend of mine had come to Christ and wished to consecrate himself and his wealth to God. He had formerly taken advantage of the government in some transactions with them. This thing came up when he was converted, and his conscience troubled him. He said, "I want to consecrate my wealth, but it seems as if God will not take it." He had a terrible struggle; his conscience kept rising up and smiting him. At last he wrote a check for $1,500 and sent it to the United

States Treasury. He told me he received a great blessing when he had done it. His conversion was bringing forth *fruit in keeping with repentance* (Matthew 3:8). I believe a great many men are crying to God for light, and they are not getting it because they are not honest.

I was once preaching, and a man came up to me after the service. He said, "I want you to notice that my hair is gray, and I am only thirty-two years old. For twelve years I have carried a great burden."

"Well," I said, "what is it?"

He looked around as if afraid someone would hear him. "Well," he answered, "my father died and left my mother with the county newspaper; that was all she had. After he died, the paper began to waste away, and I saw that my mother was fast sinking into a state of need. The building and the paper were insured for a thousand dollars, and when I was twenty years old, I set fire to the building, obtained the thousand dollars, and gave it to my mother. For twelve years that sin has been haunting me. I have tried to drown it by indulgence in pleasure and sin. I have cursed God. I have been unfaithful. I have tried to convince myself that the Bible is not true. I have done everything I could, but all these years I have been tormented."

I said, "There is a way out of that."

He inquired, "How?"

I said, "Make restitution. Let us sit down and calculate the interest, and then you pay the company the money." You should have seen that man's face light up when he found there was mercy for him. He said he would be glad to pay back the money and interest, if only he could be forgiven.

There are people today who are in darkness and bondage because they are not willing to turn from their sins and confess them. I do not know how a man can hope to be forgiven if he is not willing to confess his sins.

Bear in mind that *today* is the only day of mercy you will ever have. You can repent now and have your awful sin record blotted out. God waits to forgive you. He is seeking to bring you to Himself, but I think the Bible teaches clearly that there is *no repentance after this life*. Some people will tell you of the possibility of repentance in the grave, but I do not find that in Scripture. I have looked my Bible over very carefully, and I cannot find that a person will have another opportunity of being saved after death.

> I do not know how a man can hope to be forgiven if he is not willing to confess his sins.

Why should you ask for any more time? You have time enough to repent now. You can turn from your sins this moment, if you will. God says, *For I have no pleasure in the death of anyone who dies, declares the Lord GOD. Therefore, repent and live* (Ezekiel 18:32).

Christ said that He has *not come to call the righteous but sinners to repentance* (Luke 5:32). Are you a sinner? Then the call to repent is addressed to you. Take your place in the dust at the Savior's feet and acknowledge your guilt. Say, like the publican of old, *God, be merciful to me, the sinner,* and see how quickly He will pardon and bless you (Luke 18:13). He will even justify you and regard you as righteous by virtue of the righteousness of Him who bore your sins in His own body on the cross.

Some perhaps think they are righteous and they have no need to repent and believe the gospel. They are like the Pharisee in the parable, who thanked God that he was not as other men – *swindlers, unjust, adulterers, or even like this tax collector,* and who went on to say, *I fast twice a week; I pay tithes of all that I get.* What is the judgment about such self-righteous people? *I tell you, this man* [the poor, contrite, repenting tax collector] *went to his house justified rather than the other* (Luke 18:11-14). *There is none righteous, not even one* (Romans 3:10). *All have sinned and fall short of the glory of God* (Romans 3:23).

Let no one say he does not need to repent. Let each one take his true place – that of a sinner; then God will lift him up to the place of forgiveness and justification. *For everyone who exalts himself will be humbled, and he who humbles himself will be exalted* (Luke 14:11). Wherever God sees true repentance in the heart, He meets that soul.

I was in Colorado to preach the gospel some time ago, and I heard something that touched my heart. The governor of the state was passing through the prison, and in one cell he found a boy who had his window full of flowers that seemed to have been watched with very tender care. The governor looked at the prisoner and then at the flowers and asked whose they were. "These are my flowers," said the convict.

"Are you fond of flowers?"

"Yes, sir."

"How long have you been here?"

He told him so many years; he was in for a long sentence. The governor was surprised to find him so fond of the flowers, and he said, "Can you tell me why you like these flowers so much?"

With much emotion he replied, "While my mother was alive, she loved flowers; when I came here, I thought these would remind me of my mother."

The governor was so pleased that he said, "Well, young man, if you think so much of your mother, I think you will appreciate your liberty," and he pardoned him then and there.

When God finds that beautiful flower of true repentance springing up in a man's heart, salvation comes to that man.

Chapter 7

Assurance of Salvation

These things I have written to you who
believe in the name of the Son of God, so that
you may know that you have eternal life.
(1 John 5:13)

There are two groups of people who should not
have assurance of salvation: First, those who are
in the church but who are not converted, having never
been born of the Spirit. Second, those who are not willing to do God's will and who are not ready to follow
the path that God has mapped out for them, but want
to do their own will.

Someone will ask, "Do all God's people have
assurance?"

No; I think a good many of God's dear people have
no assurance, but it is the privilege of every child of
God to have knowledge of his own salvation beyond
a doubt. No one is fit for God's service who is filled

with doubts. If a person is not sure of his own salvation, how can he help anyone else into the kingdom of God? If I seem in danger of drowning and do not know whether I shall ever reach the shore, I cannot assist someone else. I must first get on the solid rock myself, and then I can lend my brother a helping hand. If I were blind and were to tell another blind man how to get sight, he might reply, "First get healed yourself, and then you can tell me."

> Doubt is very dishonoring to God.

I recently met with a young man who was a Christian, but he had not found victory over sin. He was in terrible darkness. Such a person is not fit to work for God, because he is overcome by his sins. He does not have victory over his doubts, because he does not have victory over his sins.

No one who is not assured of his own salvation will have time or heart to work for God. These people are busy dealing with their own problems of sin and doubt, and being burdened with their own doubts; they cannot help others to carry their burdens. There is no rest, joy, or peace – no liberty or power – where doubts and uncertainty exist.

Satan has three schemes against which we ought to be on our guard. In the first place, he uses all the forces in his kingdom to keep us away from Christ; then he devotes himself to lure us into "Doubting Castle"; but if we have a clear ringing witness for the Son of God, he will do all he can to blacken our characters and discredit our testimony.[2] Some seem to think that it is presumption not to have doubts, but doubt is very dishonoring to God. If anyone were to say that he had known a person for thirty years and yet doubted him, it would not be very believable; yet when we have known God for ten, twenty, or thirty years, doesn't it reflect on His truthful character to doubt Him?

Could Paul and the early Christians and martyrs have gone through what they did if they had been filled with doubts and had not known whether they were going to heaven or hell after they were burned at the stake? They must have had assurance.

Charles Spurgeon said:

> I never heard of a stork that, when it met with a fir tree, wondered if it had a right to build its nest there; and I never heard of a rock badger that questioned whether it were allowed to run into its rock dwelling hole. These creatures would soon perish if they were always doubting and fearing as to whether they had a right to use what God had provided for them.
>
> The stork says to himself, "Ah, here is a fir tree."
>
> He consults with his mate, "Will this do for the nest in which we may rear our young?"
>
> "Yes," she says, and they gather and arrange the

---

2   This is a reference from John Bunyan's book, *Pilgrim's Progress*, which can be purchased from Aneko Press.

materials. They never ask the question, "May we build here?" They bring their sticks and make their nest.

The wild goat on the cliff does not ask, "Do I have a right to be here?" No, he must be somewhere, and a cliff suits him, so he runs upon it.

Though these poor creatures know the provision of their God, the sinner does not recognize the provision of the Savior. He quibbles and questions, "May I?" and says, "I am afraid it is not for me," and "It cannot be meant for me," and "I am afraid it is too good to be true."

Yet nobody ever said to the stork, "Whosoever builds on this fir tree will never have his nest pulled down." No inspired word was ever said to the rock badger, "Whoever runs into this rock cleft shall never be driven out of it." If it had been so, it would make assurance doubly sure.

Yet here Christ is provided for sinners, just the sort of a Savior sinners need, and the encouragement is added, *The one who comes to Me I will certainly not cast out* (John 6:37), and *Let the one who wishes take the water of life without cost* (Revelation 22:17).

Now let us come to the Word. John tells us in his gospel what Christ did for us on earth. In his letter He tells us what Jesus is doing for us in heaven as our advocate. In John's gospel there are only two chapters where the word *believe* does not occur. With these two exceptions, every chapter in John is "Believe! Believe! Believe!" He tells us in John 20:31, *But these have been written so that you may believe that Jesus is the Christ, the Son of God; and that believing you may have life in His name.* That is the purpose for which he wrote the gospel – *that you may believe that Jesus is the Christ, the Son of God; and that believing you may have life in His name.*

In 1 John 5:13, John tells us why he wrote this letter: *These things I have written to you who believe in the name of the Son of God.* Notice to whom he writes it: *You who believe in the name of the Son of God, so that you may know that you have eternal life and that believing you may have life in His name.* There are only five short chapters in 1 John, and the word *know* occurs over forty times. It is "Know! Know! KNOW!" The key to it is "know"! All through this letter there rings out the refrain "that we might know that we have eternal life."

I went twelve hundred miles down the Mississippi in the spring some years ago, and every evening just as the sun went down, I could see men, and sometimes women, riding up to both banks of the river on mules or horses, and sometimes coming on foot, for the purpose of lighting the government lights. All down that mighty river, landmarks guided the ships' pilots in their dangerous navigation. God has given us lights or landmarks to tell us whether we are His children or not; what we need to do is to examine the signs He has given us.

In 1 John 3 are five things that we should "know." In the fifth verse, we read the first thing: *You know that He appeared in order to take away sins; and in Him there is no sin.* Not what I have done, but what He has done. Has He failed in His mission? Isn't He able to do what He came to do? Did any heaven-sent man ever fail? Could God's own Son fail? He came to take away our sins.

> Not what I have done, but what He has done.

In 1 John 3:19 is the second point to know: *We will know by this that we are of the truth, and will assure our heart before Him.* We know that we are of the truth. And if the truth make us free, we shall be free indeed. *So if the Son makes you free, you will be free indeed* (John 8:36).

The third thing to know is in the fourteenth verse: *We know that we have passed out of death into life, because we love the brethren.* The unsaved person does not like godly people, nor does he care to be in their company. *He who does not love abides in death.* He has no spiritual life.

The fourth thing worth knowing we find in verse twenty-four: *The one who keeps His commandments abides in Him, and He in him. We know by this that He abides in us, by the Spirit whom He has given us.* We can tell what kind of Spirit we have if we possess the Spirit of Christ. We will have a Christ-like spirit – not the same in degree, but the same in kind. If I am meek, gentle, and forgiving; if I have a spirit filled with peace and joy; if I am patient and gentle, like the Son of God – that is a test, and in that way we are to tell whether we have eternal life or not.

The fifth thing worth knowing, and the best of all, is found in 1 John 3:2: *Beloved, now.* Notice the word *now.* It does not say "when you die." *Beloved, now we are children of God, and it has not appeared as yet what we will be. We know that when He appears, we will be like Him, because we will see Him just as He is.*

But some will say, "Well, I believe all that, but I have sinned since I became a Christian." Is there a man or a woman on the face of the earth who has not sinned since becoming a Christian? Not one! There never has been, and never will be, a soul on this earth who has not sinned, or who will not sin, at some time in their Christian experience. But God has made provision for believers' sins. *We* are not to make provision for them; God has. Bear that in mind.

Turn to 1 John 2:1: *My little children, I am writing these things to you so that you may not sin. And if anyone sins, we have an Advocate with the Father, Jesus Christ the righteous.* John is writing to the righteous. *If anyone sins, we* – John put himself in – *we have an Advocate with the Father, Jesus Christ the righteous.* What an advocate! He attends to our interests at the very best place – the throne of God. He said, *But I tell you the truth, it is to your advantage that I go away* (John 16:7). He went away to become our high priest and also our advocate. He has had some hard cases to plead, but he has never lost one. If you entrust your immortal interests to Him, He will *make you stand in the presence of His glory blameless with great joy* (Jude 24).

The past sins of Christians are all forgiven as soon as they are confessed, and they are never to be mentioned. That is a question which is not to be opened up again. If our sins have been put away, that is the end of them. They are not to be remembered; God will not mention them anymore. This is very plain. Suppose I have a son who does wrong while I am away from home. When I return home, he throws his arms around my neck and says, "Papa, I did what you told me not to do. I am very sorry. Please forgive me."

I say, "Yes, my son," and kiss him. He wipes away his tears and goes off rejoicing.

The next day he says, "Papa, I wish you would forgive me for the wrong I did yesterday."

I would say, "Why, my son, that thing is settled, and I don't want it mentioned again."

"But I wish you would forgive me; it would help me to hear you say, 'I forgive you.'"

Would that be honoring me? Would it not grieve me to have my boy doubt me? But to gratify him I say again, "I forgive you, my son."

And if, the next day, he were again to bring up that old sin and ask forgiveness, wouldn't that grieve me to the heart? And so, my dear reader, if God has forgiven us, let's never mention the past. Let's forget those things which are behind, and reach for those which are before, and *press on toward the goal for the prize of the upward call of God in Christ Jesus* (Philippians 3:13-14). Let the sins of the past go. *If we confess our sins, He is faithful and righteous to forgive us our sins and to cleanse us from all unrighteousness* (1 John 1:9).

Let me say that this principle is recognized in courts of justice. A case came up in the courts of a country – I won't say where – in which a man had had trouble with his wife. He forgave her and afterwards brought her into court. When it was known that he had forgiven her, the judge said that the thing was settled. The judge recognized the soundness of the principle that if a sin were once forgiven, there was an end of it. And do you think the Judge of all the earth will forgive you and me and then bring up the sin again? Our sins are gone for time and eternity, if God forgives. We must confess and forsake our sins.

Now read 2 Corinthians 13:5: *Test yourselves to see if you are in the faith; examine yourselves! Or do you not recognize this about yourselves, that Jesus Christ is in you-unless indeed you fail the test.* Now examine yourselves. Try your religion. Put it to the test. Can you forgive an enemy? That is a good way to know if you are a child of God. Can you forgive an injury or take an insult, as Christ did? Can you be censured for doing well and not complain? Can you be misjudged and misrepresented and still keep a Christ-like spirit?

Galatians 5 offers another good test. Notice the fruit of the Spirit and see if you have the qualities listed. *But the fruit of the Spirit is love, joy, peace, patience, kindness, goodness, faithfulness, gentleness, self-control; against such things there is no law* (Galatians 5:22-23). If I have the fruit of the Spirit, I must have the Spirit. I could not have the fruit without the Spirit any more than an orange could exist without the tree. Jesus said, *You will know them by their fruits* (Matthew 7:16). *The tree is known by its fruit* (Matthew 12:33). Make the tree good, and the fruit will be good. The only way to get the fruit is to have the Spirit. That is the way to examine ourselves whether we are the children of God.

Another very striking passage is in Romans 8:9 where Paul says, *If anyone does not have the Spirit of Christ, he does not belong to Him.* That ought to settle the question, even though one may have gone through all the external forms that are considered necessary by some to constitute becoming a member of a church. Read Paul's life and put yours alongside it.[3] If your life resembles his, it is a proof that you are born again – that you are a new creature in Christ Jesus.

> Justification is instantaneous, but sanctification is a life work.

Although you may be born again, it will require time to become a full-grown Christian. Justification is instantaneous, but sanctification is a life work. We are to grow in wisdom. Peter says, *Grow in the grace and knowledge of our Lord and Savior Jesus Christ* (2 Peter 3:18). He also writes:

> *Now for this very reason also, applying all diligence, in your faith supply moral excellence, and in your moral excellence, knowledge, and in your knowledge, self-control, and in your self-control, perseverance, and*

3   The story of Paul's life can be found in Acts 9-28; Galatians 1:11-23; Ephesians 3; Philippians 3:3-15; 2 Timothy 4:6-8.

in your perseverance, godliness, and in
your godliness, brotherly kindness, and in
your brotherly kindness, love. For if these
qualities are yours and are increasing, they
render you neither useless nor unfruitful in
the true knowledge of our Lord Jesus Christ.
(2 Peter 1:5-8)

We are to add grace to grace. A tree may be perfect in its first year of growth, but it does not reach its full maturity that first year. It is the same with the Christian. He may be a true child of God, but not a mature Christian.

The eighth chapter of Romans is very important, and we should be very familiar with it. In the fourteenth verse the apostle says: *For all who are being led by the Spirit of God, these are sons of God.* Just as the soldier is led by his captain, the pupil by his teacher, or the traveler by his guide, so every true child of God will be led by the Holy Spirit.

Let me call your attention to another fact. All of Paul's teaching in nearly every letter rings out the doctrine of assurance. He says in 2 Corinthians 5:1, *For we know that if the earthly tent which is our house is torn down, we have a building from God, a house not made with hands, eternal in the heavens.* He had a title to the mansions above, and he says "I know it." He was not living in uncertainty. He said he had *a desire to depart and to be with Christ*, and if he had been uncertain, he would not have said that (Philippians 1:23). Then in Colossians 3:4 he says, *When Christ, who is our life, is revealed, then you also will be revealed with Him in glory.* I am told that Dr. Isaac Watts' tombstone bears this same passage of Scripture. There is no doubt at all in that verse.

Now turn to Colossians 1:12-13: *Giving thanks to the Father, who has qualified us to share in the inheritance of the saints in Light. For He rescued us from the domain of darkness, and transferred us to the kingdom of His beloved Son.* There are three "has" phrases in these verses: *has qualified us, has rescued us,* and *has transferred us.* It does not say that He is going to qualify us, that He is going to rescue us, or that He is going to transfer or change us, but that He has.

Then in Colossians 1:14: *In whom we have redemption, the forgiveness of sins.* We are either forgiven or we are not. We should not give ourselves any rest until we get into the kingdom of God, nor until we can look up and say, *For we know that if the earthly tent which is our house is torn down, we have a building from God, a house not made with hands, eternal in the heavens* (2 Corinthians 5:1).

Look at Romans 8:32: *He who did not spare His own Son, but delivered Him over for us all, how will He not also with Him freely give us all things?* If He gave us His Son, will He not give us the certainty that He is ours? I have heard the following illustration: There was a man who owed $10,000 and would have gone bankrupt, but a friend came forward and paid the sum. Later, it was learned that the man owed a few dollars more, but he did not for a moment doubt that just as his friend had paid the larger amount, he would also pay the smaller. And we have much reason for saying that if God has given us His Son, He will also freely give us all things with Him; if we want to realize our salvation beyond any doubt, He will not leave us in darkness.

Read Romans 8:33-39:

Who will bring a charge against God's elect? God is the one who justifies; who is the one who condemns? Christ Jesus is He who died, yes, rather who was raised, who is at the right hand of God, who also intercedes for us. Who will separate us from the love of Christ? Will tribulation, or distress, or persecution, or famine, or nakedness, or peril, or sword? Just as it is written, For your sake we are being put to death all day; we were considered as sheep to be slaughtered. But in all these things we overwhelmingly conquer through Him who loved us. For I am convinced that neither death, nor life, nor angels, nor principalities, nor things present, nor things to come, nor powers, nor height, nor depth, nor any other created thing, will be able to separate us from the love of God, which is in Christ Jesus our Lord.

That has the right ring in it. There is assurance for you. *I am convinced.* Do you think that the God who has justified me will condemn me? That is quite an absurdity. God is going to save us so that neither men, angels, nor devils can bring any charge against us or Him. He will have the work complete.

Job lived in a darker day than we do, but even Job said, *I know that my Redeemer lives, and at the last He will take His stand on the earth* (Job 19:25).

The same confidence breathes through Paul's last words to Timothy: *For this reason I also suffer these things, but I am not ashamed; for I know whom I have believed and I am convinced that He is able to guard what I have entrusted to Him until that day* (2 Timothy 1:12). It is not a matter of doubt but of knowledge. *I know. I am convinced.* The word *hope* is not used in the Scripture to express doubt. It is used in regard to the second coming of Christ or to the resurrection of the body. We do not say that we hope we are Christians. I do not say that I hope I am an American or I hope I am a married man. These are settled things. I may say that I hope to go back to my home or that I hope to attend a certain meeting. I do not say that I hope to come to this country, for I am here. And so, if we are born of God, we know it. He will not leave us in darkness if we search the Scriptures.

Christ taught this doctrine to His seventy disciples when they returned elated with their success, saying, *Lord, even the demons are subject to us in Your name* (Luke 10:17). The Lord seemed to restrain their enthusiasm and said that He would give them something to rejoice in. *Nevertheless do not rejoice in this, that the spirits are subject to you, but rejoice that your names are recorded in heaven* (Luke 10:20).

It is the privilege of every one of us to know beyond a doubt that our salvation is sure; then we can work for others. But if we are doubtful of our own salvation, we are not fit for the service of God.

Another passage to give us assurance is John 5:24: *Truly, truly, I say to you, he who hears My word, and believes Him who sent Me, has eternal life, and does not come into judgment, but has passed out of death into life.*

Some people say that you can never tell if you are saved until you are before the great white throne of judgment. Why, my dear friend, if your life is hid with Christ in God, you are not coming into judgment for your sins. We may come into judgment for reward. This is clearly taught where the lord dealt with the servant to whom five talents had been given and who brought

We shall be judged for our stewardship.

another five talents saying, *The one who had received the five talents came up and brought five more talents, saying, Master, you entrusted five talents to me. See, I have gained five more talents. His master said to him, Well done, good and faithful slave. You were faithful with a few things, I will put you in charge of many things; enter into the joy of your master* (Matthew 25:20-21). We shall be judged for our stewardship. That is one thing, but salvation – eternal life – is another.

Will God demand payment of the debt twice what Christ has paid for us? If Christ bore my sins in His own body on the tree, am I to answer for them as well?

Isaiah 53:5 tells us that *He was pierced through for our transgressions, He was crushed for our iniquities; The chastening for our well-being fell upon Him, and by His scourging we are healed.* In Romans 4:25 we read:

He was delivered over because of our transgressions, and was raised because of our justification. Let us believe and get the benefit of His finished work.

Then again in John 10:9: *I AM the door; if anyone enters through Me, he will be saved, and will go in and out and find pasture.* That is the promise. John 10:27-29 says:

> *My sheep hear My voice, and I know them,*
> *and they follow Me; and I give eternal life*
> *to them, and they will never perish; and no*
> *one will snatch them out of My hand. My*
> *Father, who has given them to Me, is greater*
> *than all; and no one is able to snatch them*
> *out of the Father's hand.*

Think of that! The Father, the Son, and the Holy Spirit are pledged to keep us. We see that it is not only the Father, not only the Son, but all three persons of the Triune God.

Many people want some sign in addition to God's Word. That habit always brings doubt. If I made a promise to meet a man at a certain hour and place tomorrow, and he were to ask me for my watch as a token of my sincerity, it would be a slur on my truthfulness. We must not question what God has said. He has made statement after statement and illustration after illustration. Jesus says:

> *I AM the door; if anyone enters through Me,*
> *he will be saved.* (John 10:9)

*I AM the good shepherd, and I know My own
and My own know Me.* (John 10:14)

*I AM the light of the world; he who follows
Me will not walk in the darkness, but will
have the Light of life.* (John 8:12)

Jesus said that He is *the way, and the truth, and the life*
(John 14:6). Receive Me, and you will have the truth,
for I am the embodiment of truth.

Do you want to know the way? Follow Me, and I will
lead you into the kingdom. Are you hungering after
righteousness? *I AM the bread of life; he who comes
to Me will not hunger, and he who believes in Me will
never thirst* (John 6:35).

Jesus is the living water. *Whoever drinks of the water
that I will give him shall never thirst; but the water that
I will give him will become in him a well of water springing up to eternal life* (John 4:14).

He said, *I AM the resurrection and the life; he who
believes in Me will live even if he dies, and everyone who
lives and believes in Me will never die* (John 11:25-26).

Let me remind you where our doubts come from.
A good many of God's dear people never get beyond
knowing themselves as servants. He calls us friends.
If you go into a house, you will soon see the difference between the servant and the son. The son walks
at perfect liberty all over the house; he is at home. But
the servant takes a subordinate place. We want to get
beyond servants. We ought to realize our standing with
God as sons and daughters. He will not "un-child" His

children. God hasn't only adopted us, but we are His by birth; we have been born into His kingdom. My little boy was as much mine when he was a day old as he is now at fourteen. He was my son, although it did not appear what he would be when he attained manhood. He is mine, although he may have to undergo training under tutors and teachers. The children of God are not perfect, but we are perfectly His children.

Another origin of doubts comes from looking at ourselves. If we want to be wretched and miserable, filled with doubts from morning till night, we look at ourselves. *The steadfast of mind You will keep in perfect peace, because he trusts in You* (Isaiah 26:3). Many of God's dear children are robbed of joy because they keep looking at themselves.

Someone has said, "There are three ways to look. If you want to be wretched, look within; if you wish to be distracted, look around; but if you want to have peace, look up." Peter looked away from Christ, and he immediately began to sink. The Master said to him, *You of little faith, why did you doubt?* (Matthew 14:31). He had God's eternal word, which was sure footing and better than marble, granite, or iron, but the moment he took his eyes off Christ, down he went. Those who look around cannot see how unstable and dishonoring their walk is. We want to look straight at the *author and perfecter of faith* (Hebrews 12:2).

When I was a boy, I could only make a straight track in the snow by keeping my eyes fixed upon a tree or some object before me. The moment I took my eye off the mark set in front of me, I walked crooked. It is only when we look fixedly on Christ that we find perfect peace. After He rose from the dead, He showed His disciples His hands and His feet (Luke 24:40). That was the foundation of their peace. If you want to scatter your doubts, look at the blood; if you want to increase your doubts, look at yourself. You will get doubts enough for years by being occupied with yourself for a few days.

Look at what He is and at what He has done not at what you are and what you have done. That is the way to get peace and rest.

Abraham Lincoln issued a proclamation declaring the emancipation of three million slaves. On a certain day, their chains were to fall off, and they were to be free. The proclamation was put up on the trees and fences wherever the northern army marched. A good many slaves could not read, but others read the proclamation, and most of them believed it. On that certain day, a glad shout went up: "We are free!" Some did not claim that freedom for themselves, and stayed with their old masters, but it did not alter the fact that they were free. Christ, the captain of our salvation, has proclaimed freedom to all who have faith in Him. Let us take Him at His word. The feelings of the slaves would not have made the slaves free. The power must come from the outside. Looking at ourselves will not make us free, but looking to Christ with the eye of faith will make us free.

> Looking at ourselves will not make us free, but looking to Christ with the eye of faith will make us free.

J. C. Ryle has wonderfully written in his *Faith and Assurance* tract:

> Faith, let us remember, is the root, and assurance is the flower. Doubtless, you can never have the flower without the root; but it is no less certain you may have the root and not the flower.

> Faith is that poor trembling woman who came behind Jesus in the crowd and touched the hem of His garment (Mark 5:25). Assurance is Stephen standing calmly in the midst of his murderers and saying, *I see the heavens opened up and the Son of Man standing at the right hand of God* (Acts 7:56).

> Faith is the penitent thief crying, *Jesus, remember me* (Luke 23:42). Assurance is Job sitting in the dust, covered with sores and saying, *I know that my Redeemer lives* (Job 19:25). *Though He slay me, I will hope in Him* (Job 13:15).

> Faith is Peter's drowning cry as he began to sink: *Lord, save me* (Matthew 14:30). Assurance is the same Peter declaring later before the Council, *He is the stone which was rejected by you, the builders, but which became the chief cornerstone. And there is salvation in no one else; for there is no other name under*

heaven that has been given among men by which we must be saved (Acts 4:11-12).

Faith is the anxious, trembling voice: *I do believe; help my unbelief* (Mark 9:24). Assurance is the confident challenge: *Who will bring a charge against God's elect? God is the one who justifies; who is the one who condemns?* (Romans 8:33-34).

Faith is Saul praying in the house of Judas at Damascus, sorrowful, blind, and alone (Acts 9:11). Assurance is Paul, the aged prisoner, looking calmly into the grave and saying, *I know whom I have believed* (2 Timothy 1:12), and *there is laid up for me the crown of righteousness* (2 Timothy 4:8).

Faith is life. How great the blessing! Who can tell the gulf between life and death? And yet life may be weak, sickly, unhealthy, painful, trying, anxious, worn, burdensome, joyless, and smileless to the very end.

Assurance is more than life. It is health, strength, power, vigor, activity, energy, manliness, and beauty.

A minister once pronounced the benediction in this way: "The heart of God to make us welcome, the blood of Christ to make us clean, and the Holy Spirit to make us certain." The security of the believer is the result of the operation of the Spirit of God.

Another writer says:

> I have seen shrubs and trees grow out of the rocks and overhang fearful precipices, roaring cataracts, and deep running waters; but they maintained their position and threw out their foliage and branches as much as if they had been in the midst of a dense forest. It was their hold on the rock that made them secure, and the influences of nature sustained their life. So believers are oftentimes exposed to the most horrible dangers in their journey to heaven, but as long as they are "rooted and grounded" in the Rock of Ages, they are perfectly secure. Their hold of Him is their guarantee, and the blessings of His grace give them life and sustain them in life. And as the tree must die, or the rock fall, before a dissolution can be effected between them, so either the believer must lose his spiritual life, or the Rock must crumble, before their union can be dissolved.[4]

---

4   J. Bate, as referenced in *The Biblical Illustrator* commentary on Galatians 3:7. Exell, Joseph S. "Commentary on Galatians 3:7." *The Biblical Illustrator. http://www.studylight.org/commentaries/tbi/galatians-3.html*. 1905-1909. New York.

Speaking of the Lord Jesus, Isaiah says:

> *I will drive him like a peg in a firm place,*
> *and he will become a throne of glory to his*
> *father's house. So they will hang on him all*
> *the glory of his father's house, offspring and*
> *issue, all the least of vessels, from bowls to*
> *all the jars.* (Isaiah 22:23-24)

There is one nail, fastened in a sure place, and on it hang all the instruments and all the cups. "Oh," says one little cup, "I am so small, suppose I were to drop!"

"Oh," says an instrument, "there is no fear of you, but I am so heavy, so very weighty, suppose I were to drop!"

And a little cup says, "Oh, if I were only like the gold cup there, I should never fear falling."

But the gold cup answers, "It is not because I am a gold cup that I remain up, but because I hang upon the nail."

If the nail gives way, we all come down – gold cups, china cups, pewter cups, and all; but as long as the nail stays up, all that hang on Him hang safely.

I once read these words on a tombstone: "Born, died, kept." Let us pray for God to keep us in perfect peace and assured of salvation.

Chapter 8

Christ Is All

Christ is all and in all. (Colossians 3:11)

Christ is all that we make Him to be. I want to emphasize that word *all*. Some people make Him to be *a root out of parched ground*, with *no appearance that we should be attracted to Him* (Isaiah 53:2). He is nothing to them; they do not want Him. Some Christians have a very small Savior, for they are not willing to receive Him fully and let Him do great and mighty things for them. Others have a mighty Savior, because they realize that He is great and mighty.

If we want to know what Christ wants to be to us, we must first know Him as our Savior from sin. When the angel came down from heaven to proclaim that Jesus was to be born into the world, he declared His name: *You shall call His name Jesus, for He will save His people from their sins* (Matthew 1:21). Have we been delivered from sin? Jesus did not come to save us *in* our sins but *from* our sins.

Now there are three ways of knowing a person. Some people you know only by hearsay. Others you merely know by having been introduced to them once; you know them very slightly. Still others you know by having been acquainted with them for years; you know them intimately. In the same way, I believe there are three classes of people today in the Christian church and out of it. Some know Christ only by reading

> The more we know of Christ, the more we will love Him and the better we will serve Him.

or by hearsay – those who recognize a historical Christ. Others have a slight personal acquaintance with Him. Third, some thirst, as Paul did, to *know Him and the power of His resurrection* (Philippians 3:10). The more we know of Christ, the more we will love Him and the better we will serve Him.

Savior

Let's look at Jesus as He hangs upon the cross, and let's see how He has put away sin. He came to earth that He might take away our sins. If we really know Him, we must first see Him as our Savior from sin. You remember how the angels said to the shepherds on the plains of Bethlehem, *Behold, I bring you good news of great joy which will be for all the people; for today in the city of David there has been born for you a Savior, who is*

Christ the Lord (Luke 2:10-11). Then if you go back to Isaiah, seven hundred years before Christ's birth, you will find these words: *I, even I, am the LORD, and there is no savior besides Me* (Isaiah 43:11).

In 1 John 4:14 we read: *We have seen and testify that the Father has sent the Son to be the Savior of the world.* All the heathen religions teach people to work their way up to God, but the religion of Jesus Christ is God coming down to us to save us and to lift us up out of the pit of sin. In Luke 19:10 we read that Christ Himself told the people why He had come: *the Son of Man has come to seek and to save that which was lost.* So we start from the cross not from the cradle. Christ has opened up a new and living way to the Father. He has taken all the stumbling blocks out of the way, so everyone who trusts Jesus as Savior can have salvation.

Deliverer

But Jesus Christ is not only a Savior. I might save a man from drowning and rescue him from an untimely grave, but I might not be able to do any more for him. Christ is more than a Savior. When the children of Israel were placed behind the blood, that blood was their salvation, but they would still have heard the crack of the slave driver's whip if they had not been delivered from the Egyptian yoke of bondage. It was God who delivered them from the hand of the king of Egypt.

I have little sympathy for the idea that God comes down to save us and then leaves us in prison to be the slaves of our oppressing sins. No. He has come to deliver us and to give us victory over our evil tempers, our passions, and our lusts. Are you a professing Christian but one who is a slave to some troubling sin? If you want to gain victory over that temper or that lust, continue on to know Christ more intimately. He brings deliverance for the past, the present, and the future. *Who delivered us from so great a peril of death and will deliver us; He on whom we have set our hope. And he will yet deliver us* (2 Corinthians 1:10).

Redeemer

How often, like the children of Israel when they came to the Red Sea, have we become discouraged because everything looked dark before us, behind us, and around us, and we didn't know which way to turn? Like Peter we have asked, *To whom shall we go?* (John 6:68). But God has appeared for our deliverance. He has brought us through the Red Sea into the wilderness and opened up the way into the promised land. Christ is not only our deliverer, but He is also our redeemer. That is something more than being our Savior. He has brought us back. *You were sold for nothing and you will be redeemed without money* (Isaiah 52:3). We were not redeemed *with perishable things like silver or gold* (1 Peter 1:18). If gold could have redeemed us, couldn't He have created ten thousand worlds full of gold?

Guide

When God had redeemed the children of Israel from the bondage of Egypt and brought them through the Red Sea, they struck out for the wilderness, and God became their Way. I am so thankful that the Lord has not left us in darkness as to the right way. There is no living person who has been groping in the darkness who cannot come to know the way. *I AM the way*, says Jesus (John 14:6). If we follow Christ, we shall be in the right way and have the right doctrine.

Who could lead the children of Israel through the wilderness like the Almighty God Himself? He knew the pitfalls and dangers of the way, and He guided the people through their wilderness journey into the promised land. It is true that if it had not been for their accursed unbelief, they might have crossed into the land at Kadesh Barnea and taken possession of it, but they desired something besides God's word; so they were turned back and had to wander in the desert for forty years.

I believe there are thousands of God's children still wandering in the wilderness. The Lord has delivered them from the hand of the Egyptian and would at once take them through the wilderness into the promised land, if they were only willing to follow Jesus. He has been down here and has made the rough places smooth, the dark places light, and the crooked places straight. If we will only be led by Him and follow Him, we will have peace, joy, and rest.

In the frontier, when a man goes out hunting, he

takes a hatchet with him and cuts off pieces from the bark of the trees as he goes along through the forest; this is called "blazing the way." He does it so he may know the way back, as there is no pathway through these thick forests. Christ has come down to this earth and has "blazed the way." Now that He has gone up on high, if we will only follow Him, we will be kept in the right path.

You can know if you are following Christ in this way: If someone has slandered you or misjudged you, do you treat him as your Master would have done? If you do not bear these things in a loving and forgiving spirit, all the churches and ministers in the world cannot make you right. *If anyone does not have the Spirit of Christ, he does not belong to Him* (Romans 8:9). *If anyone is in Christ, he is a new creature; the old things passed away; behold, new things have come* (2 Corinthians 5:17).

> If we will only follow Him, we will be kept in the right path.

Light

Christ is not only our way, but He is also the light upon the way. He says, *I AM the light of the world; he who follows Me will not walk in the darkness, but will have the Light of life* (John 8:12). It is impossible for any man or woman who is following Christ to walk in darkness. If your soul is in darkness, and you are groping around in the fog and mist of earth, it is because you have strayed from the true light. Nothing but light will dispel darkness. If you are walking in spiritual darkness, allow Christ into your heart. He is the light.

I remember a picture I used to like a lot, but now that I have looked at it more closely, I would not put it up in my house unless I turned the picture toward the wall. It represents Christ, standing at a door and knocking with a big lantern in His hand. You might as well hang up a lantern to the sun as put one into Christ's hand. He is the Sun of Righteousness, and it is our privilege to walk in the light of an unclouded sun (Malachi 4:2).

Peace and Joy

Many people are searching for light and peace and joy. We are not told to seek after these things. If we allow Christ into our hearts, these things will all come by themselves. I remember when I was a boy that I used to try to catch my shadow. One day I was walking with my face to the sun, and as I turned around, I saw that my shadow was following me. The faster I went, the faster my shadow followed. I could not get away from it. When our faces are directed to the Sun of Righteousness, the peace and joy are sure to come.

A man said to me some time ago, "Moody, how do you feel?" It was so long since I had thought about my feelings that I had to stop and think about it a while in order to find out. Some Christians think about their feelings all the time, and because they do not feel just right, they think their joy is all gone. If we keep our faces toward Christ and are occupied with Him, we will be lifted out of the darkness and the trouble that may have gathered around our path.

I remember being in a meeting after the Civil War broke out. The war had been going on for about six months. The army of the North had been defeated at Bull Run; in fact, we had nothing but defeat, and it looked as though the republic was going to pieces. We were cast down and discouraged. At this meeting, every speaker seemed as if he had hung his harp upon the willow (Psalm 137:2). It was one of the gloomiest meetings I ever attended. Finally, an old man with beautiful white hair got up to speak. His face literally shone. "Young men," he said, "you do not talk like sons of the King. Though it is dark here, remember it is light somewhere else." Then he went on to say that if it were dark all over the world, it was light around the throne of God.

He told us he had come from the east, where a friend had described to him how he had been up a mountain to spend the night and see the sun rise. As the party was climbing up the mountain and before they had reached the summit, a storm came on. This friend said to the guide, "I will give this up; take me back."

The guide smiled and replied, "I think we will get above the storm soon." On they went, and it was not long before they arrived at a place as calm as any summer evening. Down in the valley a terrible storm raged; they could hear the thunder rolling and see the lightning flash, but all was calm and peaceful on the mountaintop.

"And so, my young friends," continued the old man, "though all is dark around you, come a little higher and the darkness will flee away." Often when I have been inclined to get discouraged, I have thought of what he said. If you are down in the valley amid the thick fog and the darkness, get a little higher; get nearer to Christ and know more of Him.

The Bible says that when Christ died on the cross, the light of the world was put out. God sent His Son to be the light of the world, but people did not love the light because it reproved them of their sins. When they were about to put out this light, what did Christ say to His disciples? *You shall be My witnesses* (Acts 1:8). He has gone to intercede for us, but He wants us to shine for Him down here. *You are the light of the world* (Matthew 5:14). Our work is to shine, not to blow our own trumpet so people will look at us. What we need to do is to show forth Christ. If we have any light at all, it is borrowed light.

Someone said to a young Christian, "Converted! It is all moonshine!"

The young Christian replied, "I thank you for the illustration. The moon borrows its light from the sun, and we borrow ours from the Sun of Righteousness." If we are Christ's, we are here to shine for Him. By and by, He will call us home to our reward.

I remember hearing of a blind man who sat by the wayside with a lantern near him. When he was asked why he had a lantern since he could not see its light, he said it was so people would not stumble over him. I believe more people stumble over the inconsistencies of professing Christians than from any other cause. What is doing more harm to the cause of Christ than all the skepticism in the world is this cold, dead formalism, this conformity to the world, this professing what we do not possess. The eyes of the world are upon us. I think it was George Fox who said that every Quaker ought to light up the country for ten miles around him. If we were all brightly shining for the Master, those about us would soon be reached, and there would be a shout of praise going to heaven.

Truth

People say, "I want to know what is the truth." Listen: Jesus said that He is the truth (John 14:6). If you want to know what the truth is, get acquainted with Christ. People also complain that they do not have life. Many are trying to give themselves spiritual life. You may galvanize yourselves and put electricity into yourselves, so to speak, but the effect will not last very long. Christ alone is the author of life. If you want to have real spiritual life, get to know Jesus Christ. Many try to stir up spiritual life by going to meetings. That may be good, but it will be of no use unless they get into contact with the living Christ; then their spiritual life will not be an intermittent thing, but will be perpetual, flowing on and on and bringing forth fruit to God.

Keeper

Jesus is our keeper. A great many young disciples are afraid they will not stand firm and continue in the faith. *He who keeps Israel will neither slumber nor sleep* (Psalm 121:4). It is the work of Christ to keep us, and if He keeps us, there will be no danger of our falling. I suppose if the queen had to take care of the crown of England, some thief might attempt to get access to it, but it is put away in the Tower of London and guarded day and night by soldiers. The whole English army would be called out to protect it, if necessary. We have no strength in ourselves. We are no match for Satan; he has had six thousand years' experience. But then we remember that the One who neither slumbers nor sleeps is our keeper. In Isaiah 41:10 we read, *Do not fear, for I am with you; Do not anxiously look about you, for I am your God. I will strengthen you, surely I will help you, surely I will uphold you with My righteous right hand.* In Jude verse 24, we are told that He is able to keep us from falling. *We have an Advocate with the Father, Jesus Christ the righteous* (1 John 2:1).

Shepherd

Jesus Christ is also our shepherd. It is the work of the shepherd to care for the sheep, to feed them and protect them. *I AM the good shepherd. . . . My sheep hear my voice. . . . I lay down my life for the sheep.* In that wonderful tenth chapter of John, Christ uses the personal pronoun no less than twenty-eight times in declaring what He is and what He will do. In verse 28 He says, *They will never perish; and no one will snatch them out of My hand*. No person or devil is able to do it. The Scripture also declares, *Your life is hidden with Christ in God* (Colossians 3:3). How safe and how secure!

Christ says, *My sheep hear my voice . . . and they follow me* (John 10:27). A gentleman in the East heard of a shepherd who could call all his sheep to him by name. He went and asked if this was true. The shepherd took him to the pasture where they were, and he called one of them by some name. One sheep looked up and answered the call, while the others went on feeding and paid no attention. In the same way, he called about a dozen of the sheep around him. The stranger said, "How do you know one from the other? They all look perfectly alike."

"Well, you see," he said, "that sheep toes in a little; that other one has a squint; one has a little piece of wool off; another has a black spot; another has a piece out of its ear." The man knew all his sheep by their failings, for he didn't have a perfect one in the whole flock. I suppose our Shepherd knows us in the same way.

An Eastern shepherd was once telling a gentleman that his sheep knew his voice and that no stranger could deceive them. The gentleman thought he would like to put the statement to the test. He put on the shepherd's frock and turban and took his staff and went to the flock. He disguised his voice and tried to speak as much like the shepherd as he could, but he could not get a single sheep in the flock to follow him. He asked the shepherd if his sheep ever followed a stranger. He answered that if a sheep got sick, it would follow anyone.

So it is with a good many professing Christians; when they get sick and weak in the faith, they will follow any teacher that comes along; but when the soul is healthy, a Christian will not be carried away by errors and heresies. He will know whether the voice speaks the truth or not. He can soon tell the voice of God, if he is really in communion with God. When God sends a true messenger, his words will find a ready response in the Christian heart.

Christ is a tender shepherd. You may sometimes think He has not been a very tender shepherd to you, if you are passing under the rod of discipline. It is written, *For those whom the LORD loves He disciplines, and He scourges every son whom He receives* (Hebrews 12:6). That you are passing under the rod is no proof that Christ does not love you. A friend of mine lost all his children. No man could ever have loved his family more, but the scarlet fever took them one by one; all four or five children, one after another, died. The poor stricken parents went to Great Britain and wandered from one place to another, there and on the continent.

At length they found their way to Syria. One day they saw a shepherd come down to a stream and call his flock to cross the stream. The sheep came down to the brink and looked at the water, but they seemed to shrink from it, and he could not get them to respond to his call. He then took a little lamb and put it under one arm; he took another lamb and put it under the other arm, and then he went across the stream. The old sheep no longer stood looking at the water. They plunged in after the shepherd, and in a few minutes the whole flock was on the other side. He led them away to newer and fresher pastures.

As they looked on the scene, the bereaved father and mother felt that it taught them a lesson. They no longer murmured because the Great Shepherd had taken their lambs one by one into the next world. They looked up and forward to the time when they would follow the loved ones they had lost. If you have loved ones gone before, remember that your Shepherd is calling you to *set your mind on the things above, not on the things that are on earth* (Colossians 3:2). Let us be faithful to Him and follow Him while we remain in this world. If you have not taken Him for your Shepherd, do so this very day.

So Much More

Christ is not only all these things that I have mentioned. He is also our Mediator, our Sanctifier, our Justifier; in fact, it would take volumes to tell what He desires to be to every individual soul. While looking through some papers, I once read this wonderful description of Christ. I do not know where it originally came from, but it was so fresh to my soul that I would like to tell it to you:

- Christ is our Way; we walk in Him.

- He is our Truth; we embrace Him.

- He is our Life; we live in Him.

- He is our Lord; we choose Him to rule over us.

- He is our Master; we serve Him.

- He is our Teacher, instructing us in the way of salvation.

- He is our Prophet, pointing out the future.

- He is our Priest, having atoned for us.

- He is our Advocate, ever living to make intercession for us.

- He is our Savior, saving to the uttermost.

- He is our Root; we grow from Him.

- He is our Bread; we feed upon Him.

- He is our Shepherd, leading us into green pastures.

- He is our true Vine; we abide in Him.

- He is the Water of Life; we quench our thirst from Him.

- He is the fairest among ten thousand; we admire Him above all others.

- He is the brightness of the Father's glory and the express image of His person; we strive to reflect His likeness.

- He is the upholder of all things; we rest upon Him.

- He is our Wisdom; we are guided by Him.

- He is our Righteousness; we cast all our imperfections upon Him.

- He is our Sanctification; we draw all our power for a holy life from Him.

- He is our Redemption, redeeming us from all iniquity.

- He is our Healer, curing all our diseases.

- He is our Friend, relieving us in all our necessities.

- He is our Brother, cheering us in our difficulties.

- He is our Resurrection: though we die, we shall live again by Him.

- He is our Eternal Life: we shall receive the "breath of immortality" from Him.

Gotthold Lessing wrote another beautiful excerpt:

> For my part, my soul is like a hungry and thirsty child, and I need His love and consolations for my refreshment. I am a wandering and lost sheep, and I need Him as a good and faithful shepherd. My soul is like a frightened dove pursued by the hawk, and I need His wounds for a refuge. I am a feeble vine, and I

need His cross to lay hold of and wind myself
about. I am a sinner, and I need His righteousness. I am naked and bare, and I need His
holiness and innocence for a covering. I am in
trouble and alarm, and I need His solace. I am
ignorant, and I need His teaching; simple and
foolish, and I need the guidance of His Holy
Spirit. In no situation and at no time can I do
without Him. Do I pray? He must prompt and
intercede for me. Am I arraigned by Satan at
the divine tribunal? He must be my advocate.
Am I in affliction? He must be my helper. Am
I persecuted by the world? He must defend
me. When I am forsaken, He must be my sup-
port. When dying, my life; when [decaying] in
the grave, my resurrection. Well, then, I will
rather part with all the world and all that it
contains, than with You, my Savior; and, God
be thanked, I know that You, too, are neither able nor willing to do without me. You
are rich, and I am poor. You have abundance,
and I am needy. You have righteousness, and I
[have] sins. You have wine and oil, and I [have]
wounds. You have cordials and refreshments,
and I [have] hunger and thirst.

Use me then, my Savior, for whatever purpose,
and in whatever way You may require. Here is
my poor heart, an empty vessel; fill it with Your
grace. Here is my sinful and troubled soul;
quicken and refresh it with Your love. Take my

heart for Your abode; my mouth to spread the
glory of Your name; my love and all my powers for the advancement of Your honor and the
service of Your believing people. Never suffer
the steadfastness and confidence of my faith to
abate, so that at all times I may be enabled from
the heart to say, "Jesus needs me, and I Him;
and so we suit each other."

Chapter 9

Backsliding

I will heal their apostasy, I will love them freely, for My anger has turned away from them. (Hosea 14:4)

There are two kinds of backsliders. Some have never been converted; they have gone through the act of joining a Christian community and claim to be backsliders, but they never have, if I may use the expression, "slid forward." They may talk of backsliding, but they have never really been born again. They need to be treated differently from real backsliders – those who have been born of the incorruptible seed, but who have turned aside. We want to bring the latter back by the same road by which they left their first love.

Turn to Psalm 85:5-7. There you read: *Will You be angry with us forever? Will You prolong Your anger to all generations? Will You not Yourself revive us again, that Your people may rejoice in You? Show us Your lovingkindness, O LORD, and grant us Your salvation.*

Now look at Psalm 85:8: *I will hear what God the LORD will say; For He will speak peace to His people, to His godly ones; But let them not turn back to folly.*

There is nothing that will do backsliders as much good as having contact with the Word of God; for them, the Old Testament is as full of help as the New. The book of Jeremiah has some wonderful passages for wanderers. What we want to do is to get backsliders to hear what God the Lord will say.

> There is nothing that will do backsliders as much good as having contact with the Word of God

Look for a moment at Jeremiah 6:10: *To whom shall I speak and give warning that they may hear? Behold, their ears are closed and they cannot listen. Behold, the word of the LORD has become a reproach to them; They have no delight in it.* That is the condition of backsliders. They have no delight whatever in the Word of God. But we want to bring them back and let God get their ear. Now read Jeremiah 6:14-17:

> *They have healed the brokenness of My people superficially, saying, Peace, peace. But there is no peace. Were they ashamed because of the abomination they have done? They were not even ashamed at all; They did not even know how to blush. Therefore they shall fall among those who fall; At the time that I punish them, they shall be cast*

down, says the LORD. Thus says the LORD,
Stand by the ways and see and ask for the
ancient paths, where the good way is, and
walk in it; And you will find rest for your
souls. But they said, We will not walk in it.
And I set watchmen over you, saying, Listen
to the sound of the trumpet! But they said,
We will not listen.

That was the condition of the Jews when they had backslidden. They had turned away from the old paths. That is the condition of backsliders. They have got away from the good old Book. Adam and Eve fell by not listening to the word of God. They did not believe God's word, but they believed the tempter. That is the way backsliders fall – by turning away from the Word of God.

In the second chapter of Jeremiah we find God pleading with them as a father would plead with a son:

Thus says the LORD, What injustice did your
fathers find in Me, that they went far from
Me and walked after emptiness and became
empty? . . . Therefore I will yet contend with
you, declares the LORD, And with your sons'
sons I will contend. . . . For My people have
committed two evils: They have forsaken Me,
the fountain of living waters, to hew for them-
selves cisterns, broken cisterns that can hold
no water. (Jeremiah 2:5, 9, 13)

One thing we should call to the attention of

backsliders – the Lord never forsook them, but they forsook Him! The Lord never left them, but they left Him! And this, too, without any cause! He asks, *What injustice did your fathers find in Me, that they went far from Me?* Isn't God the same today as when you first came to Him? Has God changed? Men are apt to think that God has changed, but the fault is with them. Backslider, I would ask you, "What iniquity is there in God that you have left Him and gone far from Him?" You have, He says, hewed out to yourselves broken cisterns that hold no water. The world cannot satisfy the new nature. No earthly well can satisfy the soul that has become a partaker of the heavenly nature. Honor, wealth, and the pleasures of this world will not satisfy those who have gone astray and sought refreshment at the world's fountains after tasting the water of life. Earthly wells will get dry. They cannot quench spiritual thirst.

Jeremiah 2:32 says, *Can a virgin forget her ornaments, or a bride her attire? Yet My people have forgotten Me days without number.* That is the charge, which God brings against the backslider. They have *forgotten Me days without number.*

Young women have often been surprised when I have said to them, "My friend, you think more of your earrings than of the Lord."

The reply has been, "No, I do not."

But when I have asked, "Wouldn't you be troubled if you lost one, and wouldn't you look for it?"

The answer has been, "Well, yes, I think I would." But when they had turned from the Lord, it did not trouble them, nor did they seek after Him that they might find Him.

How many young women who were once in fellowship and in daily communion with the Lord now think more of their clothes and jewelry than of their precious souls! Love does not like to be forgotten. Mothers would have broken hearts if their children left them and never wrote a word or sent any memento of their affection; God pleads over backsliders as a parent over loved ones who have gone astray. He tries to bring them back. He asks: "What have I done that you have forsaken Me?"

The most tender and loving words to be found in the entire Bible are from God to those who have left Him without a cause. Hear how He argues with such: *Your own wickedness will correct you, and your apostasies will reprove you; Know therefore and see that it is evil and bitter for you to forsake the LORD your God, and the dread of Me is not in you, declares the Lord GOD of hosts* (Jeremiah 2:19).

I do not exaggerate when I say that I have seen hundreds of backsliders come back, and I have asked them if they didn't find it an evil and bitter thing to leave the Lord. You cannot find a real backslider who has known the Lord who will not admit that it is an evil and bitter thing to turn away from Him. I do not know of any verse used more to bring back wanderers than that one in Jeremiah. May it bring you back if you have wandered into the far country.

Consider Lot. Didn't he find it an evil and bitter thing? He had been in Sodom for twenty years and never once made a convert. He got on well in the sight of the world. Men would have told you that he was one of the most influential and worthy men in all Sodom. But alas! He ruined his family. It is a pitiful sight to see that old backslider going through the streets of Sodom at midnight, after he has warned his children and they have turned a deaf ear.

I have never known a man and his wife to backslide without its proving utter ruin to their children. They will make a mockery of religion and will ridicule their parents: *Your own wickedness will correct you, and your apostasies will reprove you.* Didn't David find it so? Hear him crying, *O my son Absalom, my son, my son Absalom! Would I had died instead of you, O Absalom, my son, my son!* (2 Samuel 18:33). I think it was the ruin rather than the death of his son that caused this anguish.

I remember being engaged in conversation with an old man, until after midnight several years ago. He had been wandering for years on the barren mountains of sin. That night he wanted to return to God. We prayed and prayed and prayed, until God's light broke in upon him; he went away rejoicing. The next night he sat in front of me when I was preaching, and I don't think I ever saw anyone look so sad and wretched in all my life. He followed me into the consultation room. "What is the trouble?" I asked. "Is your eye off the Savior? Have your doubts come back?"

"No, it is not that," he said. "I did not go to work, but spent all of today visiting my children. They are all married and in this city. I went from house to house, but they all mocked me. It is the darkest day of my life. I realized what I have done. I have taken my children into the world, and now I cannot get them out." The Lord had restored unto him the joy of His salvation, but there was the bitter consequence of his transgression. If you look at those around you, you can find such instances repeated again and again. Many came to your city years ago and served God in their prosperity but have forgotten Him; and where are their sons and daughters? Show me the father and mother who have deserted the Lord and have gone back to the petty elements of the world, and it is likely that their children are on the high road to ruin.

As we desire to be faithful, we warn these backsliders. It is a sign of love to warn of danger. We may be looked upon as enemies for a while, but the truest friends are those who lift up the voice of warning. Israel had no truer friend than Moses. God gave Jeremiah, a weeping prophet, to His people to bring them back to Him, but they cast off God. They forgot the God who brought them out of Egypt and who led them through the desert into the promised land. In their prosperity, they forgot Him and turned away. The Lord had told them what would happen, and it did happen (Deuteronomy 28). The king who made light of the word of God was taken captive by Nebuchadnezzar, and his children were brought before him, and every one of them was slain. Then, his eyes were put out, and he was bound in chains of brass and cast into a dungeon in Babylon (2 Kings 25:7). That is the way he reaped

> Surely it is an evil and bitter thing to backslide, but the Lord wants to win you back with the message of His Word.

what he had sown. Surely it is an evil and bitter thing to backslide, but the Lord wants to win you back with the message of His Word.

In Jeremiah 8:5 we read, *Why then has this people, Jerusalem, turned away in continual apostasy? They hold fast to deceit, they refuse to return.* That is what the Lord brings against them. *They refuse to return.* God continues:

> *I have listened and heard, they have spoken*
> *what is not right; No man repented of his*
> *wickedness, saying, What have I done?*
> *Everyone turned to his course, like a horse*
> *charging into the battle. Even the stork in*
> *the sky knows her seasons; And the turtle-*
> *dove and the swift and the thrush observe*
> *the time of their migration; But My people*
> *do not know the ordinance of the LORD.*
> (Jeremiah 8:6-7)

Now look: *I have listened and heard, they have spoken what is not right.* No family altar! No reading the Bible! No private devotion! God stoops to hear, but His people have turned away! If there is a penitent backslider, one who is anxious for pardon and restoration, you will find no words more tender than those found in Jeremiah 3:12-14:

> *Go and proclaim these words toward the*
> *north and say, Return, faithless Israel,*
> *declares the LORD; I will not look upon*

> *you in anger. For I am gracious, declares*
> *the LORD; I will not be angry forever.*
> *Only acknowledge your iniquity, that you*
> *have transgressed against the LORD your*
> *God and have scattered your favors to the*
> *strangers under every green tree, and you*
> *have not obeyed My voice, declares the*
> *LORD. Return, O faithless sons, declares*
> *the LORD; For I am a master to you, and I*
> *will take you one from a city and two from*
> *a family, and I will bring you to Zion.*

Only acknowledge your iniquity. How many times have I held that passage up to a backslider! Acknowledge your sin, and God says He will forgive you. I remember a man asking, "Who said that? Is that there?" And I showed him the passage, *Only acknowledge your iniquity,* and the man went down on his knees and cried, "My God, I have sinned." The Lord restored him then and there. If you have wandered, He wants you to come back.

Later God says, *What shall I do with you, O Ephraim? What shall I do with you, O Judah? For your loyalty is like a morning cloud and like the dew which goes away early* (Hosea 6:4). His compassion and His love are wonderful!

See Jeremiah 3:22: *Return, O faithless sons, I will heal your faithlessness. Behold, we come to You; For You are the LORD our God.* He even puts the right words into the mouth of the backslider. Only come, and if you will come, He will receive you graciously and love you freely.

In Hosea 14:1-2, 4: *Return, O Israel, to the LORD your God, For you have stumbled because of your iniquity. 2 Take words with you and return to the LORD* [He puts the words into your mouth] *Say to Him, "Take away all iniquity And receive us graciously, That we may present the fruit of our lips. . . . I will heal their apostasy, I will love them freely, For My anger has turned away from them.* "Turn back to God" rings all through these passages.

If you have wandered, remember that you left Him – He did not leave you. You must get out of the back-slider's pit in the same way you got in. If you take the same road back as when you left the Master, you will find Him now, just where you are.

If we were to treat Christ as any earthly friend, we would never leave Him, and there would never be even one backslider. If I were in a town for one week, I would not think of going away without shaking hands with the friends I had made and saying good-bye to them. I would be rightly criticized if I took the train and left without saying a word to anyone. The cry would be, "What's the matter?" But did you ever hear of a backslider telling the Lord Jesus Christ good-bye? Have you ever heard of someone turning away from Jesus who first met with God alone and said, "Lord Jesus, I have known You ten, twenty, or thirty years, but I am tired of serving You. Your yoke is not easy, nor Your burden light, so I am going back to the world, to the things of Egypt. Good-bye, Lord Jesus! Farewell"? Did

> If you have wandered, remember that you left Him – He did not leave you.

you ever hear that? No; you never did, and you never will. I tell you, if you get alone with God and shut out the world and hold communion with the Master, you cannot leave Him. The language of your heart will be, *Lord, to whom shall we go? You have words of eternal life* (John 6:68). You could not go back to the world if you treated Him in that way. You would know that you could only turn to Jesus. But you left Him and ran away. You have forgotten Him days without number. Come back today, just as you are! Make up your mind that you will not rest until God has restored unto you the joy of His salvation.

A gentleman in Cornwall once met a Christian in the street whom he knew to be a backslider. He went up to him and said, "Tell me, is there not some separation between you and the Lord Jesus?"

The man hung his head and said, "Yes."

"Well," said the gentleman, "what has He done to you?" The man answered with a flood of tears.

In Revelation 2:4-5, we read:

> *But I have this against you, that you have left your first love. Therefore remember from where you have fallen, and repent and do the deeds you did at first; or else I am coming to you and will remove your lampstand out of its place - unless you repent.*

I want to guard you against a mistake that some people make with regard to doing *the first deeds*. Many people think that they are supposed to have the same experience over again. That has kept thousands of people without peace for months, because they have been waiting for a renewal of their first experience. You will never have the same experience as when you first came to the Lord. God never repeats Himself. No two people of all earth's millions look alike or think alike. You may say that you cannot tell two people apart, but when you get acquainted with them, you can quickly distinguish differences. So, nobody will have the same experience a second time. If God will restore His joy to your soul, let Him do it in His way. Do not plan out a way for God to bless you. Do not expect the same experience that you had two or twenty years ago. You will have a fresh experience, and God will deal with you in His own way. If you confess your sins and tell Him that you have wandered from the path of His commandments, He will restore unto you the joy of His salvation.

Pay attention to the manner in which Peter fell, for nearly all people fall much the same way. I want to lift up a warning note to those who have not fallen. *Let him who thinks he stands take heed that he does not fall* (1 Corinthians 10:12). Twenty-five years ago, and for the first five years after I was converted, I used to think that if I were able to stand strong in Christ for twenty years, I would not need to be afraid of ever falling away. But the nearer you get to the cross, the fiercer the battle. Satan aims high. He went among the twelve and singled out the treasurer, Judas Iscariot, and the main apostle, Peter. Most men who have fallen have done so on the strongest side of their character. I am told that the only side upon which Edinburgh Castle was successfully assailed was where the rocks were steepest and where the garrison thought themselves secure. If any man thinks that he is strong enough to resist the devil at any one point, he needs special watch there, for the tempter comes that way.

Abraham stands at the head of the family of faith, and the children of faith may trace their lineage to Abraham; yet down in Egypt, he denied his wife (Genesis 12). Moses was noted for his meekness, yet he was kept out of the promised land because of one hasty act and speech, when he was told by the Lord to speak to the rock so that the congregation and their beasts should have water to drink. *Listen now, you rebels; shall we bring forth water for you out of this rock?* (Numbers 20:10).

> We who are followers of Christ need to pray constantly to be made humble and kept humble.

Elijah was remarkable for his boldness, and yet he went off a day's journey into the wilderness like a coward and hid himself under a juniper tree, requesting that he might die, because of a message he received from a woman (1 Kings 19). Let's be careful. No matter who the man is – he may be in the pulpit or some other high place – if he becomes conceited, he will be sure to fall. We who are followers of Christ need to pray constantly to be made humble and kept humble. God made Moses's face to shine so that other men could see it, but Moses himself did not know that his face shone. The more holy in heart a person is the more clear his Christ-like daily life and love for God will be seen by the outer world. Some people talk about how humble they are, but if they have true humility, they will not need to announce it. A lighthouse does not have to beat a drum or blow a trumpet in order to proclaim that it is near; it is its own witness. If we have the true light in us, it will show itself. Those who make the most noise are not the ones who have the most piety.

There is a brook, or a little "burn" as the Scotch call it, not far from where I live. After a heavy rain you can hear the rush of its waters a long way off; but let there come a few days of pleasant weather, and the brook becomes almost silent. There is also a river near my house, the flow of which makes little noise, and it continues on in its deep and majestic course all year long. We should have so much of the love of God within us that its presence will be evident without our loud proclamation of the fact.

The first step in Peter's downfall was his self-confidence. The Lord warned him. The Lord said, *Simon, Simon, behold, Satan has demanded permission to sift you like wheat; but I have prayed for you, that your faith may not fail* (Luke 22:31-32). But Peter said, *Lord, with You I am ready to go both to prison and to death!* (Luke 22:33). *Even though all may fall away because of You, I will never fall away* (Matthew 26:33). "James and John and the others may leave You, but You can count on me!" But the Lord warned him: *I say to you, Peter, the rooster will not crow today until you have denied three times that you know Me* (Luke 22:34).

Though the Lord rebuked him, Peter said he was ready to follow Him to death. That boasting is too often a forerunner of a downfall. Let us walk humbly and softly. We have a great tempter, and in an unguarded hour, we may stumble and fall and bring a scandal on Christ.

The next step in Peter's downfall was that he went to sleep. If Satan can rock the church to sleep, he does his work through God's own people. Instead of Peter watching one short hour in Gethsemane, he fell asleep. The Lord then asked, *So, you men could not keep watch with Me for one hour?* (Matthew 26:40). The next thing was that he fought in the energy of the flesh. The Lord rebuked him again and said, *Those who take up the sword shall perish by the sword* (Matthew 26:52). Jesus had to undo what Peter had done.

> It is a sad thing when a child of God follows afar off.

The next thing, *Peter was following Him at a distance* (Matthew 26:58). Step by step he moves away. It is a sad thing when a child of God follows afar off. When you see him associating with worldly friends and throwing his influence on the wrong side, he is following afar off. It will not be long before disgrace will be brought upon the old family name, and Jesus Christ will be wounded in the house of his friends. The man, by his example, will cause others to stumble and fall.

After that, Peter is familiar and friendly with the enemies of Christ. A damsel says to this bold Peter:

"You too were with Jesus the Galilean."
But he denied it before them all, saying, "I
do not know what you are talking about."
When he had gone out to the gateway,
another servant-girl saw him and said to
those who were there, "This man was with
Jesus of Nazareth." And again he denied
it with an oath, "I do not know the man."
(Matthew 26:69-72)

Another hour passed, and Peter still did not realize his position. When another person confidently affirmed that Peter's speech gave him away as being a Galilean, he was angry and *began to curse and swear*, and again denied his Master; and the cock crew (Matthew 26:73-74).

Peter started high on the pinnacle of conceit, and went down step by step until he broke out into cursing and swore that he never knew his Lord.

The Master might have turned to him and said, "Is it true, Peter, that you have forgotten Me so soon? Don't you remember when your wife's mother lay sick of a fever, and I rebuked the disease and it left her (Mathew 8:14-15)? Don't you remember your astonishment when you caught so many fish that you exclaimed, *Go away from me Lord, for I am a sinful man* (Luke 5:8)? Do you remember when in answer to your cry, *Lord, save me*, I stretched out My hand and kept you from drowning in the water (Matthew 14:30-31)? Have you forgotten when, on the Mount of Transfiguration with James and John, you said to Me, *Lord, it is good for us to be here; if You wish, I will make three tabernacles here* (Matthew 17:4)? Have you forgotten being with Me at the supper table and in Gethsemane? Is it true that you have forgotten Me so soon?" The Lord might have upbraided him with questions such as these, but He did nothing of the kind. He cast one look at Peter, and there was so much love in it that it broke that bold disciple's heart; he went out and wept bitterly.

After Christ rose from the dead, notice how tenderly He dealt with the erring disciple. The angel at the sepulchre said, *Tell his disciples and Peter* (Mark 16:7). The Lord did not forget Peter, though Peter had denied Him three times, and He caused this kind and special message to be conveyed to the repentant disciple. What a tender and loving Savior we have!

> What a tender and loving Savior we have!

Friend, if you are one of the wanderers, let the loving look of the Master win you back. Let Him restore you to the joy of His salvation.

Before closing, let me say that I pray that God will restore some backslider who reads these pages and may become a useful member of society and a bright ornament of the church in the future. We would never have had the thirty-second Psalm if David had not been restored: *How blessed is he whose transgression is forgiven, Whose sin is covered!* (Psalm 32:1). If not for God's love, we would not have that beautiful fifty-first Psalm, which was written by the restored backslider. Nor would we have had that wonderful sermon on the day of Pentecost when three thousand were converted – preached by another restored backslider (Acts 2).

May God restore other backsliders and make them a thousand times more useful for His glory than they ever were before. If you do not know Jesus or if you have wandered from Him, look to Him today!

About the Author

Dwight Lyman Moody was born on February 5, 1837, in Northfield, Massachusetts. His father died when Dwight was only four years old, leaving his mother with nine children to care for. When Dwight was seventeen years old, he left for Boston to work as a salesman. A year later, he was led to Jesus Christ by Edward Kimball, Moody's Sunday school teacher. Moody soon left for Chicago and began teaching a Sunday school class of his own. By the time he was twenty-three, he had become a successful shoe salesman, earing $5,000 in only eight months, which was a lot of money for the middle of the nineteenth century. Having decided to follow Jesus, though, he left his career to engage in Christian work for only $300 a year.

D. L. Moody was not an ordained minister, but was an effective evangelist. He was once told by Henry Varley, a British evangelist, "Moody, the world has yet to see what God will do with a man fully consecrated to Him." Moody later said, "By God's help, I aim to be that man."

It is estimated that during his lifetime, without the help of television or radio, Moody traveled more than one million miles, preached to more than one million people, and personally dealt with over seven hundred and fifty thousand individuals.

D. L. Moody died on December 22, 1899.

Moody once said, "Some day you will read in the papers that D. L. Moody, of East Northfield, is dead. Don't you believe a word of it! At that moment I shall be more alive than I am now. I shall have gone up higher, that is all – out of this old clay tenement into a house that is immortal; a body that death cannot touch, that sin cannot taint, a body fashioned like unto His glorious body. I was born of the flesh in 1837. I was born of the Spirit in 1856. That which is born of the flesh may die. That which is born of the Spirit will live forever."